Rapidly Changing Securities Markets

Zicklin School of Business Financial Markets Series

Robert A. Schwartz, Editor
Zicklin School of Business
Baruch College/CUNY
New York, NY, USA

More information about this series at http://www.springer.com/series/7133

Robert A. Schwartz • John Aidan Byrne
Eileen Stempel
Editors

Rapidly Changing Securities Markets

Who Are the Initiators?

Springer

Editors
Robert A. Schwartz
Zicklin School of Business
Baruch College/CUNY
New York, NY
USA

John Aidan Byrne
Rockaway, NJ
USA

Eileen Stempel
Zicklin School of Business
Baruch College/CUNY
New York, NY
USA

Zicklin School of Business Financial Markets Series
ISBN 978-3-319-54587-5 ISBN 978-3-319-54588-2 (eBook)
DOI 10.1007/978-3-319-54588-2

Library of Congress Control Number: 2017946319

Printed on acid-free paper

This Springer imprint is published by Springer Nature
The registered company is Springer International Publishing AG
The registered company address is: Gewerbestrasse 11, 6330 Cham, Switzerland

Preface

Rapidly Changing Securities Markets: Who Are the Initiators?

Opening Remarks[1]

Robert Schwartz
Zicklin School of Business, Baruch College, CUNY
New York, USA

Robert Schwartz: Nothing can be better for a conference than sharp debate and conflict. Today I am anticipating a good and vibrant debate. Having said that, let me be a little feisty. I am hearing a lot of good things being said about how our markets have evolved over the years. In many ways, our electronic markets of today are indeed a big improvement over the nonelectronic markets of 15 years ago. Of late, however, I have also been hearing increasing negativity about our market structure. I hear that asset managers are not finding it so easy to execute their big orders. I find this ironic: We have high-frequency trading, we have minuscule latency, and still it can take hours to execute a large order completely.

Markets are more fragile today. I have heard concern that retail customers have lost confidence in the fairness of the markets, and in their stability. How good, we should ask, is market quality for mid- and small-cap stocks? So often in these proceedings, we talk in the abstract with big caps implicitly in our minds. How about the mid and small caps? This is a big, big issue. And how about capital raising in the primary markets?

---

[1] Readers should note that some of the commentary in these Opening Remarks, for the 2012 Baruch College conference, is integrated at the beginning of Chapter 1, "The SEC's Order Handling Rules of 1997 and Beyond: Perspective and Outcomes of the Landmark Regulation," Richard Lindsey, John Aidan Byrne, and Robert A. Schwartz, *Journal of Portfolio Management*, Spring 2016, reprinted with permission of the *Journal of Portfolio Management*. This paper is based on an address by Richard Lindsey at the same 2012 conference.

The session I will be moderating at 9:30 am this morning is titled, "How do the Markets Look 15 Years after the 1997 Order Handling Rules?" My friends, two things happened in 1997: The order handling rules were enacted, and I left NYU's Stern School of Business and came to Baruch. Some contrasts can be made. In the ensuing years, NASDAQ, the NYSE, and Baruch have all been fundamentally reengineered. My going to Baruch has turned out to be a great decision for me, and I am delighted to be here. Moreover, with all the change in the industry, with all the perpetually unanswered questions, I believe that I could keep on running these Baruch conferences forever. It is amazing how the discussions keep going on and on.

Exchanges have privatized. Baruch as a part of CUNY has not. Sometimes I think we should have, and sometimes I think the exchanges should not have. We have a fantastic new building, the one you are sitting in right now. When I got to Baruch in 1997, this site was a big hole in the ground. Across the street from the big hole in the ground, on the first floor of our Library Building, seeds were being sewn that led to the development of our Wasserman Trading Floor-Subotnick Financial Services Center, home of what I will call the best business school trading room in the country. Down at 11 Wall Street… oh my god, what happened to the Big Board's trading floor? We have greatly strengthened our faculty with excellent new hires. Gosh, what happened to NASDAQ's dealer market?

These are other contrasts. How about transparency? Well, I am not telling you. Like a dark pool, my mouth is shut on this one. How about fragmentation? Baruch hasn't fragmented, and we have gotten far more competitive on a national level. The equity markets? We now have 13 public exchanges and over 40 ATSs! Wow, what a change on this score since I got to Baruch. The clock ticks slowly in academia. It can take years to produce a research paper, and then it can take a year or more to get it accepted for publication. For sure, we in academia know all about latency. Our equity markets are on the opposite end of the spectrum. In our electronic markets today, time is measured in milliseconds. Fast is good but when is fast too fast? I know that we will be talking a lot about this today.

So, everybody, let's get started.

List of Participants

Name	Company	Title
Janet Angstadt	Katten Muchin Rosenman LLP	Partner
Stephen Bookbinder	GreenCrest Capital	Global Head of Sales
Harold Bradley	The Ewing Marion Kauffman Foundation	Former Chief Investment Officer
Kevin Callahan	AX Trading Network	CEO
Doug Clark	ITG Canada Corp., ITG, Inc.	Managing Director, Research
Chris Concannon	Virtu Financial	Partner
Tom Gira	FINRA	Executive Vice President and Head of Market Regulation
Bill Harts	Harts and Company	President
Frank Hatheway	NASDAQ OMX	Chief Economist
George Kledaras	FIX Flyer	Chairman
Cheryl Knopp	Liquidnet	Co-Head of Corporate Strategy/ Liquidnet Private Shares
David Krell	International Securities Exchange	Chairman
Richard Lindsey	Callcott Group LLC	CEO
Timothy J. Mahoney	BIDS Trading L.P.	CEO
Joseph M. Mecane	NYSE Euronext	Executive Vice President, Head of US Equities
Nina Mehta	Bloomberg News	Reporter
William O'Brien	Direct Edge	CEO
Michael Pagano	Villanova University	Professor of Finance
Kenneth Pasternak	KABR Real Estate	Chairman
Joe Ratterman	BATS Global Markets, Inc.	Chairman, President, and CEO
Brett Redfearn	J.P. Morgan Securities	Head of Market Structure Strategy
Keith Ross	PDQ Enterprises LLC	CEO
Robert A. Schwartz	Zicklin School of Business, Baruch College, CUNY	Speiser Professor of Finance

(continued)

Robert Shapiro	Bloomberg Tradebook LLC	Head of Trading and Execution Consulting
Jeffrey Sprecher	Intercontinental Exchange, Inc.	Chairman of the Board and Chief Executive Officer
Adam Sussman	TABB Group	Head of Research
Neal Wolkoff	American Stock Exchange	Former CEO/Chairman

Conference Sponsors

BATS Exchange
BIDS Trading
Bloomberg Tradebook LLC
Direct Edge
Intercontinental Exchange
International Securities Exchange
ITG Inc.
Liquidnet
NASDAQ OMX
NYSE Euronext
PDQ ATS Inc.
TABB Group

Contents

Preface: Rapidly Changing Securities Markets: Who Are the Initiators? v

List of Participants vii

Conference Sponsors ix

Chapter 1 : The SEC's Order Handling Rules of 1997 and Beyond: Perspective and Outcomes of the Landmark Regulation 1

Chapter 2 : Fifteen Years After the Order Handling Rules, How Do the Markets Look Today? 15

Chapter 3 : Competition, Incentives, and Innovations in the Great American Marketplace 33

Chapter 4 : Regulators and Innovators as Initiators 45

Chapter 5 : A Walk Through Time 61

Chapter 6 : New Initiators: Technology, Market Events, and Business Practices 81

Chapter 7 : The Need for Further Change 97

Chapter 8 : History, Regulation, and the Evolution of a World-Class Exchange 113

Chapter 1
The SEC's Order Handling Rules of 1997 and Beyond: Perspective and Outcomes of the Landmark Regulation

Richard Lindsey, John Aidan Byrne, and Robert A. Schwartz

The Securities and Exchange Commission's Order Handling Rules (OHRs) of 1997 ushered in a period of fundamental and unprecedented change in the competitive structure of the US equity markets. Most significantly, the OHRs led to the reengineering of NASDAQ's dealer market. The new rules required market makers (1) to display customer limit orders in their quotes, (2) to display these quotes in the NASDAQ quote montage whenever they have placed more aggressively priced customer quotes in an electronic communications network (ECN), or else (3) to update their own quotes in NASDAQ to match the ECN quotes. In discussing these rules, Schwartz and Francioni (2014) put it this way:

> The proverbial cat was out of the bag. The new requirements set the stage for the electronic communications networks to enter the field. Before the rules were instituted, Instinet was the one and only ECN. By September 1999 there were nine. [2004]

On a December evening in 1996, in a large hotel ballroom in lower Manhattan, the lead author of this paper (Lindsey) took the stage to face several hundred NASDAQ broker-dealers. Another author (Schwartz) was in the audience. The scene was certainly historic. In his courageous presentation, Lindsey outlined the details of the proposed OHR regulation. The import of the message was etched on the anxious faces of those present. After his presentation had concluded, these same people filed quietly out of the ballroom. Only the shuffling of their footsteps broke the eerie silence.

R. Lindsey (✉)
Callcott Group LLC, New York, NY, USA

J.A. Byrne
Rockaway, NJ, USA

R.A. Schwartz
Zicklin School of Business, Baruch College/CUNY, New York, NY, USA

R.A. Schwartz et al. (eds.), *Rapidly Changing Securities Markets*,
Zicklin School of Business Financial Markets Series,
DOI 10.1007/978-3-319-54588-2_1

In the nearly two decades since the 1997 Order Handling Rules were introduced, the equity markets have experienced tremendous technological innovation, intensified competition between an expanding set of alternative trading venues, and further regulatory change. How has market quality responded? What further structural and regulatory changes are still required? These were among the key questions addressed at the Baruch Conference.[1]

To be sure, nothing is better for the success of a conference than robust debate and creative conflict. That said, let us be a little feisty here. Positive things are said about how our markets have evolved over the years. In many ways, our electronic markets today are a huge improvement over their non-electronic predecessors. Lindsey's presentation at the Baruch Conference described many of these valuable changes. Nevertheless, other voices have expressed negativity and doubt about elements of our market structure. For example, it is noted that asset managers are finding it difficult to execute their large orders.[2] Electronic markets can be fragile (to wit, the May 6, 2010, Flash Crash). Moreover, retail customers' confidence in the stability and fairness of the markets appears to have been shaken. How good, one might then ask, is market quality for mid- and small-cap stocks? And how about capital raising in the primary markets?

The major developments since 1997 are not, of course, attributable exclusively to the Order Handling Rules. The previously noted technological change, the evolving competitive landscape, and further regulatory initiatives are also major causal factors. So too are the exchanges' transitions from membership organizations to for-profit enterprises, alongside the expanding globalization of trading.[3] In the next section of this paper, we consider the pressures for change that faced the markets in the years leading up to the institution of the 1997 Order Handling Rules.

The Pressures for Change

At the time of the Baruch Conference, the S&P 500 index was roughly six times the level it had been 25 years earlier. We deliberately selected 25 years prior as a starting point because that was roughly 1 year after the 1987 Market Crash.[4] Because the crash was such a disruption in the market, it spurred many subsequent changes,

[1] This chapter is a slightly amended paper of the same title by Richard Lindsey, John Aiden Byrne and Robert A. Schwartz, published in the *Journal of Portfolio Management*, Spring 2016. The paper was developed from Lindsey's Opening Address at this 2012 Baruch Conference in New York City. Reprinted with permission from the *Journal of Portfolio Management*.

[2] This is a bit ironic. We have high-frequency trading and miniscule latency, but it can still take hours to completely execute a large order.

[3] A timeline of major market changes, starting with Instinet's launch in 1969, is presented in Exhibit 1.

[4] The Stock Market Crash of 1987 or "Black Monday" on October 19, 1987, was the largest one-day market crash in history. The Dow lost 22.6% of its value, or $500 billion dollars.

ranging from mechanizing trading systems to improving our market structure. But much more went on behind the scenes than people ever realized.

The events of the past quarter century have been studied closely in market microstructure papers. In academia, market microstructure, which studies how markets should work and be designed, has become a growth industry. Unfortunately, however, some of the academic literature can be slightly misinformed or misguided.

For example, in the 1990s, most academic thinking held that, when a market order went to a dealer, the order would be routed for execution to the best quote in the market, regardless of which dealer displayed that quote. In other words, dealer markets were thought to be highly competitive. But that is not the way the markets worked. When your market order went to a dealer *and* your dealer happened to have the best quote, your order was executed at that price. Otherwise, your order might not have been executed at all – or it might have been executed later at an inferior price, even though better prices were available in the market when the order was submitted. Dealers kept their order flow to themselves and didn't really compete with each other on price to attract order flow. Dealers did not route customer orders to other, competing dealers for execution. In short, markets did not work the way academics thought.

In the 1990s, academics began to focus on how investors should (and did) interact with the market – that is, how they actually bought and sold securities. In that process, the academics discovered that there were hidden costs associated with transacting in the markets. And institutional investors began to take this research to heart. They realized that they should care about the bid-ask spread, that they should care about market impact[5] and implementation shortfall,[6] and that they should care about how markets actually worked. All of these costs mattered because they affected the performance of their investment portfolios. When institutional investors actually began to care about these things and became proactive, the market started to change, and it did so simply because the largest customers were demanding change.

But it should be kept in mind that the real driver of market innovation has always been technology. Markets cannot stand in the way of technology. History shows that incumbent markets usually try to fight those changes, but in the end they do not succeed.

Let's turn the clock back a little – to 1969. That was the year Instinet began, representing, perhaps, the first electronic marketplace for stock trading in the USA. Two years later, in 1971, NASDAQ, an electronic dealer market in stocks, was launched. Because of these and other changes then on the horizon, in 1975 Congress

[5] "Market impact" refers to the impact of a decision to buy or to sell a security as reflected in the extent to which the buying or selling shifts the prices against the buyer or seller.

[6] "Implementation shortfall" refers to the difference between the current price or value when a decision is made to buy or sell a security and the final execution price or value, factoring in commissions, fees, and taxes. In sum, implementation shortfall is the total of the execution costs and the opportunity cost in the instance of adverse market movement between the time of the trading decision and order execution.

enacted amendments to the Securities Exchange Act of 1934.[7] In part, the amendments emphasized the important and evolving role of technology in US markets, and, in so doing, they charged the SEC with linking markets and enhancing competition. Twelve months later, the Cincinnati Stock Exchange went fully electronic. The Toronto Stock Exchange became an electronic market in 1977. We had the first electronic linkage between markets the following year in the form of the Intermarket Trading System (ITS).[8] While people talk about linkages today, we should recognize that it was really some time ago that markets began to link together.

But not all of this worked the way it was envisioned, particularly in the case of the Intermarket Trading System, ITS. In fact, the ITS was purposely designed not to work particularly well because the markets designed it! The exchanges did not want orders routed from their own exchange to another exchange for execution – the easiest way to prevent that was to make sure that the ITS linkage was slow and awkward to use.

The concept of control over order flow still holds today. Whether we are talking about exchanges, dealers, or electronic execution systems, intermediaries want to control the order flow. This involves segmenting flow that is desirable to execute against, crossing flow deemed less desirable through proprietary "dark pools" or other systems, and, as a last resort, routing that flow elsewhere through a linkage.

Embedded in the 1975 Amendments mentioned earlier was the National Market System (NMS). The NMS was supposed to ensure implementation of five points that Congress had decided were necessary to strengthen the markets: (1) economically efficient execution, (2) fair competition, (3) widespread availability of information regarding quotes and transactions, (4) orders executed in the best market, and (5) an opportunity for investors' orders to be executed without dealer participation. Look at our markets today – as an industry, we are still struggling to implement these five points.

Why? Because these five ideals are somewhat antithetical to the way market intermediaries like to operate. Market intermediaries are not interested in getting out of the way of orders – that is, allowing orders to simply interact with each other. It is hard to make much money if you just let orders interact with each other. Intermediaries make much more if they trade against orders – at least certain orders. Exchanges, dealers, brokers, etc., make their money by standing between investors who are buying and investors who are selling. That is not to say that these intermediaries do not provide anything valuable to investors, but the question remains, is the value worth the cost?

---

[7] Federal legislation launched on June 4, 1975, to amend the Securities Exchange Act of 1934. The 1975 amendments instructed the Securities and Exchange Commission to cooperate with the industry in creating a National Market System along with an ambitious system for the clearance and settlement of securities transactions nationwide. The amendments also provided for the prohibition of fixed-commission rates, promulgated earlier by the SEC in its Rule 19b-3.

[8] The Intermarket Trading System, ITS, was created to electronically link the trading floors of the regional exchanges in trading stocks listed on either the NYSE or AMEX and one or more of the regionals. The Cincinnati Stock Exchange was among the first regionals to use the ITS.

Some Questions Never Change

For those who have been involved with market structure for a long time, the same questions or issues tend to be repeated over the years. Sometimes the questions may be the same because people do not like to hear the answers – so they keep asking the same questions, hoping for an answer that they like. But the answers are almost always the same. They may change slightly when something is modified in the market to address a specific issue or problem, but, eventually, the system adapts and we end up back with many of the same issues – they just manifest themselves somewhat differently.

Consider, for example, dark pools.[9] Lately, there has been a lot of discussion in the press about dark pools. The first dark pool started in 1986 (although it was not called that at the time). It was Instinet's after-hours cross, where after-hours orders could be routed for execution with complete anonymity (including as to whether or not the order even existed). This was long before the term "dark pool" entered our lexicon. Same theme, different time.

Or consider market fragmentation. At the turn of the nineteenth century, there were more than 100 stock markets in the USA.[10] Do you not think that the markets were fragmented back then? This raised the same questions that are debated today. Over the years, many of those markets closed and consolidated. Why? Because technology changed, because technology allowed investors in Kansas City or Des Moines to send, almost instantaneously, their orders to an exchange that was hundreds or thousands of miles away. And technology allowed exchanges to compete in new ways and with lower costs. That is why we can think of technology as the primary innovator in markets.

There were a number of changes in the 1990s, and we will touch on some of the high points. The Manning Rule was introduced in 1994,[11] and it was the first time that market makers were actually prohibited from executing ahead of their customers' limit orders. If a market maker's customer placed an order, the Manning Rule required the market maker to give any better price in the market to the customer rather than execute that order for the market maker's own account. Previously, market makers would often take the better price for themselves (for example, buy at a lower price) and then execute the customer's order at a worse price (selling to the customer the same security at a higher price). In 1994, Christie and Schultz published their seminal paper on price collusion on the NASDAQ market. A year later, in 1995, markets moved to T + 3 settlement.[12] Then, in 1996, the SEC issued a 21(a)

[9] In dark pool electronic trading, pre-trade prices are not displayed, thus explaining the term "dark." and the price at which shares are exchanged are only revealed post-trade.

[10] See 1963 Special Study, p. 928, or Coffee (2002).

[11] The Manning Rule prohibited dealers from trading ahead of a customer order.

On September 12, 2011, Rule 5320 replaced existing FINRA customer limit and market order protection rules ("Manning"), NYSE Rule 92 and similar exchange rules.

[12] Settlement occurs 3 days (3) after the transaction date (T).

report on the NASDAQ market and a settlement with the NASDAQ market makers on collusion and quote-fixing.[13]

The SOES Bandits should also be mentioned.[14] They were traders who used NASDAQ's Small Order Entry System (SOES) to trade quickly. The earliest high-frequency traders actually started in the 1990s as SOES Bandits, with many of them surviving today as high-frequency traders. Many of the questions or arguments that were raised then are still being asked today. Clearly, some participants in markets do not like speed, while some do.

In general, market participants will always try to obtain an advantage. For some, that advantage is found in speed – whether it be the SOES Bandits of the 1990s or the high-frequency traders of the 2000s. The demand for speed also helped to drive the application of technology in our markets, as high-speed traders became an important source of order flow for the exchanges.

Decimalization, the Order Handling Rules, and Regulation ATS

Let us next consider the pricing convention on NASDAQ, as described in the Christie and Schultz (1994) paper. The authors focused on the avoidance of odd eights by dealers in their published quotes – and they got it almost right. In reality, dealers only avoided odd eights when the dealer spread in the market was greater than three quarters. There were actually two pricing conventions that the dealers used. They avoided quoting odd eights when the dealer spread was greater than three quarters, and they avoided odd sixteenths when the dealer spread was less than three quarters.

The Christie-Schultz paper started the ball rolling by asking the question: "Is there collusion in the NASDAQ market?" The SEC looked into that question – and their investigation resulted in an enforcement action against the NASDAQ market makers, in the Justice Department's actions against the NASDAQ market makers, and, finally, in the SEC's 1997 Order Handling Rules.

The Order Handling Rules were intended to be a structural fix for the lack of competition that existed in the dealer market. The idea was to strengthen competition in the marketplace for both market makers and exchanges. The OHRs ultimately

[13] Report Pursuant to Section 21(a) of the Securities Exchange Act of 1934 Regarding the NASD and the NASDAQ Market. See http://www.sec.gov/litigation/investreport/nasdaq21a.htm

[14] "SOES Bandits" were the bane of many NASDAQ market makers who frequently accused these early high-speed electronic traders of unfairly profiting from less nimble market makers who could "lose" heavily in the short time it took them to adjust their two-sided quotes.

See also Michael Berryhill, Watch out, stock market, here come the SOES BANDITS, *Houston Post*, June 13, 1996. http://www.houstonpress.com/news/watch-out-stock-market-here-come-the-soes-bandits-6571504

led to the concept of Electronic Communication Networks (ECNs)[15] and, finally, to Regulation Alternative Trading Systems (Reg ATS).[16] Why were these changes necessary? Roughly speaking, in excess of 80% of all the securities traded in the NASDAQ market followed the pricing conventions just mentioned.

So it was not just a little corner of the market; it was the majority of the OTC market. The structural fixes implemented by the Order Handling Rules – which essentially required display, dissemination, and the ability to interact with customer limit orders – broke the pricing conventions used in the NASDAQ market. After these conventions were broken, spreads that for years had been inexplicitly wider in the NASDAQ market than the NYSE almost immediately collapsed and became very close to NYSE spreads. Although the OHRs had the most significant effect on NASDAQ, the NYSE and other exchanges that were also required to comply experienced a narrowing spreads as well.

Around this time, the markets started moving to decimal pricing (or penny increments) in the quotes. Many people seem to think that the SEC required the markets to move to decimals or that the SEC was told to do it by Congress. Neither is correct, although it is true that there was something called the Common Cents Pricing Act of 1997.[17] The Act was circulated in the House but was never even voted on in Committee. It was written by David Cavicke, who was on the staff of Representative Mike Oxley.[18] There is a part that states that stocks should be quoted in dollar and cents; however, stocks were already quoted in dollars and cents, and perhaps what he really wanted to say is that stocks should be priced in decimals, pennies, or something similar. But Cavicke did not change his language. In any event, it did not really matter because the bill did not go anywhere.

So let us consider some of the backstory about how decimals were introduced into the marketplace. In 1997, the NYSE was using its regulatory arm to pressure some of their member firms because those firms were routing orders (which could have been executed on the exchange) to the third market – that is, to OTC dealers who made markets in NYSE-listed securities. Third-market market makers were paying for order flow, and exchange members were routing to those third markets because of those payments. The NYSE, in the guise of a regulator, would basically say to those members: "Why are you routing to the third market? That cannot be best execution – you should be routing those orders to the exchange." The implication being that there might be an enforcement action if the orders were not routed to the NYSE.

---

[15] For example, in 1997, Josh Levine and Jeff Citron created Island ECN. A year later, Island ECN accounted for as much as 15% of Nasdaq trades.

[16] See RIN 3235-AH41

Regulation of Exchanges and Alternative Trading Systems, https://www.sec.gov/rules/final/34-40760.txt Release No. 34–40,760; File No. S7-12-98.

[17] See S. 838 (is) – Common Cents Stock Pricing Act of 1997. http://www.gpo.gov/fdsys/pkg/BILLS-105s838is/content-detail.html

[18] Michael G. Oxley, former Republican Congressman for the 4th District of Ohio (1981–2007), was Chairman of the House Financial Services Committee during office. Oxley achieved wide-acclaim for his co-authorship of the landmark Sarbanes-Oxley Act of 2002.

One of those third-market market makers called one of us (Lindsey) and said, "You know Dick Grasso[19] is doing this, and if he doesn't stop beating up on the firms and taking business away from me, I am going to break the eighth and quote in sixteenths." This was the reply: "Go ahead, call him and tell him that." He did, but the NYSE did not stop their pressure tactics. So Bernie Madoff[20] – yes, that Bernie Madoff – called Lindsey back a few weeks later and said, "Dick hasn't stopped; I am going to break the eighth and start quoting in sixteenths."

So, it was Bernie Madoff who broke the eighth – the pricing convention that had been in place for the NYSE for over 200 years! Madoff had programmed his system well in advance to trade in decimals and sixteenths. He went to sixteenths first and the Street went crazy. Within a few weeks the market was, of course, trading in sixteenths. After sixteenths, it did not take long to move to decimals. Systems needed to be modified, and eventually the exchanges submitted rules for trading in decimals that were approved by the SEC in the 2000s. Of course, at the time, the USA was the only market in the world that did not have decimal pricing – every other equity market in the world traded in decimals.

Let us next pick up on Reg ATS. There may be some confusion between ATSs and ECNs. The difference is that an ECN is run by a broker/dealer or, potentially, by an exchange. In other words, an ECN is run by a regulated entity. An ATS, on the other hand, is run by something that is neither a broker/dealer nor an exchange. The reason the concept of an ATS and its regulation was created is because, following the establishment of a regulatory framework for ECNs, the thinking got extended further. There was nothing, for example, that would have prevented Microsoft from setting up an electronic market to trade Microsoft stock. And if Microsoft or any other company did that, there was nothing in the regulatory structure to ensure that transparency, fairness, and access would be built into that market. The idea behind Reg ATS was to close that little regulatory loophole – so if an otherwise unregulated entity set up a trading system, there would be a way for the SEC to have regulatory authority.

Quoted spreads came down with the move to decimals, and the across-stock volume weighted average number of shares quoted also decreased. Frank Zarb, who was the Chairman of NASDAQ in the late 1990s, publically recognized that ECNs developed because the exchanges really were not fulfilling investor's needs. And that realization spurred the growth of ECNs, which were bringing in new technology, new order types, and new competition. The goal with the Order Handling Rules and Reg ATS was to introduce more competition into the market.

[19] Richard "Dick" Grasso, the legendary former Chairman and CEO of the New York Stock Exchange from 1995 to 2003. He was forced out in a public controversy over his compensation package. Grasso rose from humble beginnings in Jackson Heights, Queens, NY, joining the Big Board as a clerk in the late 1960s, climbing the ranks to helm the exchange at its height. Grasso's departure in 2003, after a 36-year career at the exchange, resulted from an outcry over his reported pay package of about $140 million. On July 1, 2008, the New York State Supreme Court of Appeals dismissed all claims in this regard against Grasso.

[20] Founder of Bernard L. Madoff Investment Securities, better known publicly for later perpetrating what is regarded as the largest Ponzi scheme in financial history.

The Commission never considered it to be its job to decide what that competition needed to look like. It did not think it should force a particular market structure (like a Central Limit Order Book[21]). Quite simply, the Commission believed that competition between execution venues should drive the development of markets.

Have All the Impacts Been Beneficial?

Let us examine some of the issues that people raise when they say that the changes arising from the Order Handling Rules – decimalization and automation – have been bad for the markets. First, the number of public customer accounts of broker/dealers has grown approximately 80% since 1997. Equity ownership by individuals has decreased, but ownership among institutional investors has increased. Institutions play a larger role today in the marketplace. But this was a trend that started during World War II, so there is nothing new there. The literature has shown that institutional trading costs have come down by almost every measure, including commissions and implementation shortfalls. Even average retail commissions have come down during the past decade. That is clearly good for investors. Broker commission income has actually increased over time because volumes have increased – obviously; that is good for brokers.

Another comment one might hear is how the average trade size on the NYSE has diminished over this time period. Personally, I would question that. If one looks at average trade size on the NYSE over a longer period of time, one will see a nice big run up in trade size from the 1980s to the late 1990s, with a peak in 1988. But average trade size today is not much different from that of the 1970s. If one might complain that the trade size is smaller than it was in 1990, that is definitely true, but perhaps misleading.

In September 1990, there was a rule change (Rule 115A) at the NYSE that modified the way opening trades were reported. Instead of opening trades being reported as a single, large block, the rule required that the reporting be based on the individual orders that constituted the block. Thus, the opening trade was reported as a number of small trades, instead of a single, large trade size.

Although changing the way trades are reported does not change overall volume, it does change average trade size dramatically, because the opening generally constitutes the largest volume of the day. The Rule 115A change is one of the reasons the data show a decline in trade size since 1990. There may be other factors that influence reported trade size, but we need to be careful when we try to draw conclusions without understanding and accounting for all of those factors.

Execution speed has definitely increased. Most would consider this to be a positive. The median displayed depth (at least for larger stocks) has gone up, but it has not

[21] A CLOB would centralize limit orders across the marketplace, a concept proposed by US regulators in the past but opposed by various interests.

changed very much for the smaller-cap stocks.[22] In other words, for the most liquid stocks, there has been an increase in displayed depth (especially if you include depth displayed plus or minus 6 cents outside the best bid or offer). But, for less liquid stocks, there has not been much of a change in displayed depth.

As of October 2012, the time of the Baruch Conference, the average holding time for equities was on the order of a year. That is the average holding time across equities and across investors, so that number includes the holding times of high-frequency traders. Average holding time for stocks has decreased over the last decade – but if you look back before the 1929 crash, holding time is about the same today as it was then. What we see is a long period of higher average holding times for equities beginning after the 1929 crash and running through the late 1970s, with average holding times steadily declining since then.

There are many explanations for such an observation. For example, stocks did not trade very actively during the Great Depression or during World War II. Stocks held by individuals at that time were sold over the intervening years (1940–1980) to institutional investors like pension funds, mutual funds, and life insurance companies which may have had longer holding periods. Today, there appears to be much more active trading in equities across the board – even for institutional investors. The pressure to achieve returns drives much of this activity, and it increases the turnover of equities.

Clearly, the market shares of exchanges have changed dramatically over time because there has been more competition. Presumably, the New York Stock Exchange or NASDAQ would consider this to be a bad result, but others can see it simply as a result of competition. You can also see where that order flow is going. Not surprisingly, despite the complaints, the order flow really is not being siphoned off to dark pools, and it is not being siphoned off to all these ATS (Alternative Trading Systems). Instead, the most rapidly growing "execution venue" right now is *internalization*.[23] Most of that order flow is actually going to internalization and the dealer systems. For those who have been around a while, that is nothing new. The desire to control order flow is simply manifesting itself today in a different way.

That is not to say that there are not some issues with the way markets function today. Obviously, electronic trading is very much in our thoughts and on the pages of the press. There are clearly issues associated with algorithms – and whether there are sufficient controls in the market to ensure that an algorithm has been properly tested and cannot disrupt trading. There is the issue of high-frequency trading, which may be abusive in some forms. There are undoubtedly some forms of high-frequency trading that do not add depth (liquidity) to the market, but instead attempt to manipulate prices.

[22] See Angel et al. (2010).

[23] The Securities and Exchange Commission offers this explanation on its website: "When you place an order to buy or sell a stock, your broker has choices on where to execute your order. Instead of routing your order to a market or market-makers for execution, your broker may fill the order from the firm's own inventory. This is called "internalization." In this way, your broker's firm may make money on the "spread" – which is the difference between the purchase price and the sale price."

Co-location[24] is not new. We have always had co-location in our markets; simply think about the floor traders and specialists at the NYSE. To a large extent, we do not have all those traders standing co-located on the exchange floor anymore. Instead, we have computers sitting next to one other, serving the same purpose that people did in the past. Granted, computers are faster than people. Granted, they have to be programmed properly. But, at the same time, this can be seen as just another example of technology driving the markets.

Conclusion

If you go back in history, you can see all the same fights that we are experiencing today. They happened when the telegraph and the telephone came to the market and disrupted vested interests. In the late nineteenth century, the NYSE painted its windows black to prevent anybody from distributing prices outside the floor of the NYSE, so that all prices could be controlled inside.

Go back to the Buttonwood Tree agreement.[25] The 24 brokers who signed the agreement promised to give preference to each other in all negotiations for the purchase and sale of stock. The activities that people engage in the market, and the types of complaints that result from those activities, are no different today than they were 20, 40, or 100 years ago.

Consider the following quotes taken from a letter written by Robert W. Haack, Chairman of the NYSE in 1970, complaining to the SEC:

> Some traders deliberately instruct brokers to execute orders on regional exchanges or take their business to the third market in order to conceal their activity from the public view.
>
> It is an unusual and interesting phenomenon that the market with the greatest degree of regulation, greatest capital, and the most impressive record for depth and liquidity should find itself being fragmented. I believe that the causes for this fragmentation are not related to any change in the unique economies of scale available on the Floor of the New York Stock Exchange but to the presence of antiquated and unequal rules and the emergence of a new environment for trading in securities.
>
> I am also concerned about the lack of regulation in the recently developed 'computer markets' which are highly susceptible to abuse and non-disclosure.
>
> The New York Stock Exchange, to put it crassly, no longer has the only game in town. The result has been a break in the similarity of interests between people engaged in floor activities, whose profitability depends on the share of business brought to our Exchange, and firms doing business with the public, who have become willing partners to fragmentation.

---

[24] This refers to the ability of market participants to gain advantages in the speed of their trade executions and price-quote data through advanced technology, specifically the "co-location" of their computer servers near stock exchanges' computers. That lowers so-called latency, a critical factor in high-speed trade executions. The practice is regarded as legal though it has many critics.

[25] The New York Stock Exchange began on May 17, 1792, with the signing of the Buttonwood Agreement by 24 New York City stockbrokers and merchants outside 68 Wall Street under a Buttonwood tree.

Haack was complaining about fragmented markets, about other markets stealing order flow from the NYSE, about computerized trading and its impact on the NYSE and order flow, about dealers internalizing orders away from the NYSE, and about market participants who wanted to keep order flow hidden. Sound familiar?

It is the same story over and over. In Exhibit 1, we have briefly outlined a history of US market structure, paying particular attention to the 1997 Order Handling Rules and the developments that followed. In so doing, we have stressed the importance of competition, and we note that, with competition, some enterprises survive and some do not. That said, let us end with Lindsey's concluding remark at the October 2012 conference:

> I went to the SEC as an economist. I am still an economist. I still believe in free markets and competition. I did write laws and rules, but they were intended to spur competition. Because I believe that competition regulates markets better than regulation ever can.

Exhibit 1: Timeline of Major Market Changes

1969 Instinet Launched
1971 NASDAQ Starts
1975 Amendments to the '34 Act
1976 Cincinnati Stock Exchange goes fully electronic
1977 Toronto Stock Exchange begins electronic trading
1978 ITS links the exchanges
1982 NASDAQ starts in ITS
1984 SuperDOT
Mid-1980s Program Trading
1984 SOES
1986 First Dark Pool – Instinet After-Hours Cross
1986 London goes electronic
1987 POSIT
1987 Reuters buys Instinet
1987 Market "Break"
1987 NASDAQ ACES allows market maker auto-execution
1990 NASDAQ Selectnet
1991 NYSE begins after-hours crossing system
1992 NYSE volume surpasses 200 million
1992 NYSE 200th anniversary
1994 Manning Rule
1994 NASDAQ volume surpasses NYSE
1994 Christie and Schultz
1995 T + 3 Settlement
1996 21(a) Report
1996 SEC & Justice Department Settlement with Nasdaq Market Makers
1997 Order Handling Rules
1997 NASDAQ & NYSE begin trading in sixteenths

1997 NYSE first billion share day
1998 Reg ATS
1998 Island trades 15% NASDAQ Volume
1998 Optimark Launched
1999 ISE Launched
1999 Gramm-Leach Bliley repeals Glass-Steagall
2000 Decimalization of NYSE
2000 Rule 390 Abolished
2000 NYSE Direct + auto-execution launched
2001 NYSE 2.81 billion share day
2001 NASDAQ sells to firms
2001 NASDAQ Decimalized
2001 Disclosure of Order Execution and Routing Practices
2002 NASDAQ Super Montage
2003 Dick Grasso Resigns from NYSE
2004 Specialist Firms settle with SEC
2005 Reg NMS Approved
2005 Exchange/ECN Consolidation. (Nasdaq/INET & NYSE/ARCA)
2005 NASDAQ trades publically
2005 HF Trading Explodes
2005 Record price for NYSE seat $3.25 million
2005 Goldman Sigma X and other broker ATSs
2005 Knight buys ATTN (Houtkin) and rebrands direct edge
2006 NYSE/Archipeligo/Euronext Merger
2006 NYSE trades publically
2006 BATS inverts pricing
2007 Reg NMS fully implemented
2007 Flash Orders
2007 Uptick Rule Removed
2008 Dark Pools take off
2008/2009 Short Sale Restrictions
2009 Suspension of Flash Orders
2010 SEC Concept Release on Equity Market Structure
2010 Sponsored Access Rules
2010 Flash Crash
2010 Direct Edge becomes Stock Exchange

Acknowledgments On October 9, 2012, Baruch College's Financial Markets Conference Series presented, "Rapidly Changing Securities Markets: Who Are the Initiators?" One major initiator was Richard Lindsey, former Director of Market Regulation at the Securities and Exchange Commission. Lindsey was the chief architect and an intellectual *tour de force* of the Commission's landmark 1997 Order Handling Rules. This article, with additional research, is an expansion of his presentation at that Baruch Conference.

References

Anand A, Irvine P, Puckett A, Venkataraman K (2010) Market crashes and institutional trading. Working paper

Angel J, Harris L, Spatt C (2010) Equity trading in the 21st century. Working paper

ASX (2010) Algorithmic trading and market access arrangements

ASX Group (2011) Submission to ASIC consultation on equity market structure regulatory framework

Barclay M, Christie W, Harris J, Kandel E, Schultz P (1999) Effects of market reform on the trading costs and depths of Nasdaq stocks. J Financ 54(1):1–34

Bennett P (2003) Who needs stock exchanges? Working paper

Blume M (2012) The structure of the US equity markets. Working paper

Brattle Group (2011) Trading at the speed of light

Brown W, Mulherin J, Weidenmier M (2008) Competing with the New York stock exchange. Q J Econ 123(4):1679–1719

Christie W, Schultz P (1994) Why do Nasdaq market makers avoid odd-eighth quotes. J Financ 49:1813–1840

Chordia T, Roll R, Subrahmanyam A (2008) Liquidity and market efficiency. J Financ Econ 87(2):249–268

Coffee J (2002) Competition among securities markets. Working paper

GAO (2005) Decimal pricing has contributed to lower trading costs and a more challenging trading environment

Haack R (1970) Competition and the future of the New York Stock Exchange. Speech at the Economic Club of New York

Hasbrouck J, Sofianos G, Sosebee D (1993) New York Stock Exchange systems and trading procedures. NYSE working paper 93–01

Hendershott T, Jones C (2005) Island goes dark: transparency, fragmentation, and regulation. Rev Financ Stud 18:743–793

Hendershott T, Jones C, Menkveld A (2008) Does algorithmic trading improve liquidity? Working paper

O'Hara M, Ye M (2009) Is market fragmentation harming market quality? Working paper

RBC Global Asset Management (2012) US market structure: is this what we asked for? Working paper

SEC (1963) Report of special study of the securities markets

SEC (1996) Report pursuant to section 21(a) of the securities exchange act of 1934 regarding the NASD and the NASDAQ market

Rydqvist K, Spizman J, Strebulaev I (2008) The evolution of aggregate stock ownership: a unified explanation. Working paper

Schwartz R, Francioni R (2014) Equity markets in action. Wiley, New York

Smith R (2010) Is high-frequency trading inducing changes in market microstructure and dynamics? arXiv:1006.5490v1

Werner I (2002) Institutional trading costs on Nasdaq: have they been decimated? Nasdaq working paper

Weston J (2000) Competition on the Nasdaq and the impact of recent market reforms. J Financ 55:2565–2598

Zhu H (2012) Do dark pools harm price discovery? Working paper

Chapter 2
Fifteen Years After the Order Handling Rules, How Do the Markets Look Today?

Robert Schwartz, Doug Clark, David Krell, Kenneth Pasternak, and Adam Sussman

Robert Schwartz This panel fits well with the splendid presentation earlier this morning by Richard Lindsey.[1] It will take us back to the groundbreaking Order Handling Rules[2] introduced in 1997. Which reminds me of a famous meeting Rich helmed on Wall Street in lower Manhattan in 1996. It was in the auditorium of a big hotel, and it occurred right before the Order Handling Rules were enacted. I didn't see any armed guards in the hotel lobby, despite the outrage among some market practitioners present about the proposed rules! In fact, I was the only one to defend Rich in a room full of a couple hundred angry NASDAQ market makers!

I recall Rich giving his presentation, spelling out what was expected under the rules. After the meeting, when I walked out the door with the market makers, was it

[1] See Chapter 2: Opening Address – Equity Market Structure and Regulation: The Last 25 Years. Richard Lindsey, Chief Investment Strategist, Janus Liquid Alternatives.

[2] The Order Handling Rules included the Limit Order Display and the Quote Rules that paved the way for today's "modern" high-speed electronic markets, starting with the early wave of upstart Electronic Communications Networks, or ECNs. See Securities and Exchange Commission, Order Execution Obligation, http://www.sec.gov/rules/final/37619a.txt

R. Schwartz
Zicklin School of Business, Baruch College, CUNY, New York, NY, USA

D. Clark (✉)
ITG Canada Corp., ITG, Inc., Toronto, ON, Canada

D. Krell
International Securities Exchange, New York, NY, USA

K. Pasternak
KABR Group, Ridgefield Park, NJ, USA

A. Sussman
TABB Group, New York, NY, USA

R.A. Schwartz et al. (eds.), *Rapidly Changing Securities Markets*, Zicklin School of Business Financial Markets Series,
DOI 10.1007/978-3-319-54588-2_2

ever so quiet. Not a single person said a word. So, it is very fitting that you, Rich, are our first keynote speaker today. What a hell of an initiator you were. You spirited us into a new environment, into a new world.

Despite so much change in the regulatory and technological environment, it is amazing how the issues remain unchanged through the years. We are in a competitive marketplace. Whether you compete by using more technology or less, it doesn't really change the reality of competition, especially in a continuous trading environment. That said, I would like to hear the thoughts of my panel about the two key initiators, that is, technology and innovation. I will start with Doug Clark of ITG. Ian Domowitz of ITG is not here, but he gave me this memorable quote: "A lot of good has been done, but the place has gone crazy," Ian said of our market structure. Was he drinking [laughter]? What would you like to say about that Doug? As you think about the answer, I will give you another word Ian used to describe our market structure today – "dysfunctional." The markets are dysfunctional.

Can we agree not to get into a philosophical debate about dysfunctional? It is like liquidity or illiquidity; you know it when you see it. Let's just leave it at that.

Doug Clark I am not going to disagree immediately with Ian. He is higher up the food chain than me at ITG!

Schwartz Pretending he isn't, what would you say?

Clark Pretending he isn't, I am certainly not going to shy away from being provocative! The overall question today is about the strength of our market structure. More specifically, who are all the instigators; are the markets more fragile? Everything becomes more fragile when you add technology. Look at cars that drive at a speed of 5 miles per hour, they can't really do a lot of damage so you don't need airbags; you don't need antilock brakes when you have cars that can be driven at 140 miles per hour. In other words, once you introduce more speed into the marketplace, then we definitely become more fragile. As you add complexity, you do the same thing. My car today is far more complex mechanically than a 1962 Chevy. I can't lift the hood of my car today with the idea I will easily know what to do with the engine underneath. I don't have the same control over a car as I would have had with a vintage model. If something goes wrong I have to call the shop. I can't even pretend I am going to fix it.

But today's car is typically far better than the golden oldies. The car will last longer; it will get me there faster; it is more powerful. But there is some downside. There is absolutely a downside in our markets today. There are certainly issues, and we have to be careful. We have to understand the unintended consequences of all the rule changes. How many people here can say they truly understand all the order types available in the US equity market? I would be surprised if there was a single person in the US that understood every equity order type. It is very difficult.

What is Hide Not Slide[3]? Who knows? So it is very difficult for the buy-side trader, for the actual investor, to understand what is going on in the marketplace. And if you can't understand what is going on with your money, you are going to be a little less likely to hand it over and trade it.

At the same time, Ian would show you that transaction cost analysis research demonstrates very clearly that implementation shortfall[4] costs are down. The market has become more efficient. So there are a lot of good developments in the market structure as well as a lot of bad. There is an underlying narrative that our markets are broken. That narrative is stretched. It is unfortunate that there are some people on TV telling us that our markets are broken.

A great example came last week when we saw a 120-s blip in a single name, Kraft foods.[5] Suddenly there was a story about it in *The Wall Street Journal*, and there was a 20-min segment on CNBC about how our markets are broken because a single name had a 120-s blip. That is not a broken market. That is a single incident.

We saw a significant correction in India's stock exchange last week related to a manual order entry. So this fragile situation is there whether you have electronic or manual markets. As markets become faster, and as people have the ability to trade orders in a faster time frame, you are going to have these moves. They will happen more quickly. There is more complexity. There is less understanding.

Regarding the Flash Crash,[6] it took us something like a year to understand what happened there. There are people who still don't understand what happened. We have to make sure we educate people, not just the institutional investor, but also the retail public about what is happening in the market. But overall I would say our markets are better today.

---

[3] Hide Not Slide was an order type invented by Direct Edge, before it became part of BATS Global Markets. And it was at the center of controversy when BATS settled, for a reported $14 million, charges with federal regulators in early 2015 on allegations it did not properly describe this order type and other types to customers of its two exchanges, EDGA and EDGX. The name Hide Not Slide refers to the idea of "hiding" a stock from display, rather than "sliding" it to a lower price, often by a penny, as occurs for other, albeit visible orders.

[4] Difference between the current price or value when a decision is made to buy or sell a security and the final execution price or value, factoring in commissions, fees, and taxes. In sum, implementation shortfall is the total of the execution costs and the opportunity cost in the case of adverse market movements between the time of the trading decision and order execution.

[5] Price of the stock (NASDAQ: KRFT) surged 25% within 1 min soon after the market opened. The glitch was blamed on a broker error by NASDAQ that affected multiple exchanges. "Investors were hit with another stock-trading glitch Wednesday, this one in a household name – Kraft Foods – which saw dozens of trades canceled when a broker error caused shares to soar shortly after the opening bell," according to *The Wall Street Journal*. See *WSJ* story, Kraft Hit by Trading Glitch, October 3, 2012, Alexandra Scaggs and Matt Jarzemsky.

[6] The Flash Crash occurred on Thursday, May 6, 2010, when the Dow Jones Industrial Average declined by about 9% and then quickly recouped those losses within minutes. At the time, it was the second largest point swing, 1010.14 points, and the biggest 1-day point decline, 998.5 points, on an intraday basis, in the history of Dow Jones Industrial Average.

Schwartz I am hearing about investors losing confidence. Is that something they just always say, the retail customers in particular? What is your reaction to that, and why did Ian say, 'The place is going crazy'? You can pass on that if you prefer. I don't want to force you to answer for Ian.

Clark When you see investors walk away from the market, everybody looks for reasons. The idea that it is investor confidence in the structure of our markets, as opposed to the macro events, is overstated. When I talk to institutional portfolio managers, they are not trading as much as they used to. It is not because they don't understand the order types or are scared about co-location.[7] It is because they don't know what is happening in Europe. They don't understand what is happening with the debt ceiling; or they have no certainty over the US elections. I don't think it is related to some new order type that BATS introduced, or to a new data feed from Direct Edge. Is the market going crazy?

The rate of change, both regulatory and coming from the exchanges, is troubling. I certainly can't speak with any certainty of what happened at Knight on August 1. I would suggest it probably had to do with different coding changes they had to make in a short period of time. They had 3 weeks to get up and running for the RLP, or Retail Liquidity Provider program.[8] They tried to be there on day 1. Maybe that was a mistake. But there are so many changes you must try to understand. One may work. But when you add three other changes on top of that, all of a sudden you find that it doesn't work. That is the real concern about technology. How do you carefully make all these changes in a short period of time?

Adam Sussman I agree. Rationally, there is no way market structure could be impacting investor confidence. When a small issue like Kraft turns into a story in *The Wall Street Journal*, it can impact investor confidence. Let me share a story: Sitting down with my mother two nights ago, she says, "I was reading about dark pools – that is where insider trading occurs right?" I mean when my mom, an ordinary investor on Main Street, is asking me questions like that, it points to the fact market structure is impacting investor confidence in some way.

Schwartz Adam, how did you answer her? Did you say yes or no?

Sussman Actually, I tried to explain it to her and then her eyes rolled over, so I said yeah, let's talk about the kids!

---

[7]This refers to the ability of market participants to gain advantages in the speed of their trade executions and price-quote data through advanced technology, specifically the "co-location" of their computer servers near stock exchanges' computers. That lowers the so-called latency, a critical factor in high-speed trade executions. The practice is regarded as legal though it has many critics.

[8]This electronic turmoil violently impacted the accuracy of prices in 140 stocks listed on the New York Stock Exchange on August 01, 2012, further hurting already fragile investor confidence in the soundness of US stock markets.

"Knight Capital's CEO Tom Joyce confirmed that 'a very large software bug' was the source of yesterday's market fiasco," according to an exclusive interview with Bloomberg TV on its Market Masters program this morning. See Knight's CEO Admits Software Bug Was Cause of Market Mayhem, Ivy Schmerken, *Wall Street & Technology*, August 2, 2012.

Schwartz I well understand.

Sussman I don't think we should underestimate the impact those negative stories are having on investors. It would be foolish of us to ignore them. I agree that they shouldn't be having an impact. But these negative stories actually are having an impact with the industry under the spotlight.

Clark I don't disagree. That is part of it – we are under a spotlight. There is an existing narrative. If you look at August 1, by 10:00 in the morning there were people on TV speculating on what had happened. I will tell you, anybody on TV at 10:00 on August 1 who didn't work for Knight, speculating about what had happened, actually had no idea what happened. They were only on TV because they could go along with the existing narrative. They had a belief in what they thought the market was doing. They had books to sell on how the markets are broken.[9] So they were on TV saying the markets are broken. They had no idea if the markets were broken. They had no idea that it was a single incident, a coding bug, an exchange bug. They had no way of knowing.

Unfortunately, when you get an existing narrative like that, the media hops on board – and they exaggerate it. So there is that issue. But if you talk to a lot of investors, I don't think they are going to say, I don't like that order type, I don't like that data feed.

Sussman Yes, well they don't get into the details.

Kenneth Pasternak I might have a different standing in conversation with people. I wear two hats – as an investor and in many people's eyes I have some insight.[10] But I would confess to you here that I don't have any particular insight that is less than 10 years old. I don't have a book to sell. I would disagree a bit about everybody's narrative here.

Look at market participation – a lot of people got a very severe dose of reality and had a lack of confidence about whether they were qualified to be self-directed investors or individual holders of stock in 2008.[11] They have never come back into the market. Which brings us to the highly publicized market structure anomalies. These really have nothing to do with investing.

Let's be honest. If you talk to E*Trade, you know that the average capital committed is under $2000 and that the average order size is around 200 shares. I can

[9] Appropriately, here is one book that was published in 2012 and released prior to the Kraft incident: *Broken Markets*. How High Frequency Trading and Predatory Practices on Wall Street Are Destroying Investor Confidence and Your Portfolio. *Sal Arnuk & Joseph Saluzzi* (FT Press).

[10] In 1995, Pasternak co-founded Knight Trading Group in 1995 along with Walter Raquet. Pasternak served as the company's CEO from 1995 until he retired on January 21, 2002. It was the predecessor organization of the same Knight Capital Group Inc. discussed on the panel. At the time of writing, Pasternak was the founder and executive chairman of The KABR Group and also the managing principal of Chestnut Ridge Capital.

[11] The Dow Jones Industrial Average scaled its pre-recession, all-time high on October 9, 2007, closing at 14,164.43. Less than 18 months later, through 2008, it had declined more than 50% to 6594.44 on March 5, 2009.

assure you that 3 or 4 cents on either side of the share price isn't going to dictate somebody's investing philosophy, especially when the average holding period is 1 year. From a person who is an investor in stocks, the asset class has really fallen out of favor. I know it is not market structure. It has never gotten back in favor despite the rally we had off the bottom. That is a different conference topic – why investors have so far failed to return to the asset class during a pretty good stock market rally. The answer is not market structure.

Schwartz I am hearing that market structure is not making things worse. But we have had a lot of change; we have a lot more application of technology. I could reverse my question and ask, why hasn't it made it that much better? Could you speak to that? Then I want to turn to you David, because, as we all know, you have yourself made a tremendous impact on market structure in the options market – and you might have a very different perspective on this topic given the instruments you trade. Ken, please talk first about technology.

Pasternak You can talk about technology and market structure. You are an economist. Unfortunately, I went to a state school, I was an Ed. major who had a minor in business, so I am not well versed.

Schwartz Where is this school?

Pasternak It has a great business school today. It is the State University in New Paltz. Nonetheless, I have read on various topics of economic thought. In fact, there is more innovation in the market. The high-frequency traders are a great example of a market evolving. Here we have people seeing economic opportunity, possibly to the detriment of good market structure. That may have a few different elements worth considering, including depth in market and price improvement. But volumes today are, nevertheless, much higher than they have ever been compared with when I left the business 10 years ago. Unfortunately, you might say that it is not the kind of participants today that one might want. But this reality is, nevertheless, undeniable today against the backdrop of one of the worst recessions in my lifetime.

You have an almost 1400 Dow today – so to say that market structure is inhibiting investors, or the value of the stock market, is not accurate. In fact, the market is up 25% in the past year. If you look at the facts – they just don't support the theory that market structure is broken. I compare it to an airplane and an air crash – and my wife won't fly for the past 5 years. But, in fact, going on an airplane is the safest mode of transportation in the world. I think walking is 10 or 20 times more dangerous than air travel. But there is a good portion of the population that is petrified to get onto a plane. You have to look at facts versus behaviors.

Schwartz David, what would you like to say as a chief initiator here? We need more instigators, but you are an initiator!

David Krell Richard Lindsey started off with a very good historical perspective on the last 25 years – and that is exactly where I would like to begin. Next week it will be October 19, which would be, I hate to call it, the anniversary of the market break in 1987 which Richard talked about.[12] I was working in the options business at the New York Stock Exchange at that time – and I was on the floor that day. And for those of you who don't remember, the market was down 508 points, some 22% on that 1 day. The institutional investors panicked. Remember this was pre-Internet, pre all the hoopla on CNBC that you see every day – so the public didn't panic until later that evening, and the next morning, when they heard it on the news.

As Richard said, that led to a lot of reforms in the marketplace. It ushered in a whole list of things at the NYSE. They introduced market-wide circuit breakers, which are still in existence. And, of course, that led to the Order Handling Rules a decade later. I am sure we will talk later about individual circuit breakers that are now being proposed, speed bumps and so forth. The competition the government wanted actually occurred with the proliferation of ATSs and ECNs, new trading venues, and so on.

I agree with Richard. Two elements were fundamentally important in the changes that occurred in the market – computer speeds and network speeds. The ISE[13] wouldn't be in existence without the enabling technology – and the network speeds that then became available – when we started trading in 2000. We would not have been able to launch trading, say a decade earlier, if that technology wasn't ready.

In addition to the technology, what occurred in the marketplace was also driven by the regulatory changes that came from the desire to eliminate the abuse that occurred in the trading room – as a result of price-fixing that Richard talked about. The competition that Richard talked about came in part from regulatory change, such as the introduction of tick sizes of sixteenths and then penny's in 2000.[14]

One thing that hasn't yet been mentioned: Because they didn't have natural liquidity, ECNs and the ATSs introduced rebates into the process. Market participants were encouraged by being paid to rest their orders on the book. That is now also causing a lot of this high-frequency trading to occur. Because people can put in a bid, buy at that bid and get paid to put that bid in – and they don't have to wait to sell the offer at the higher price, they can sell at the same price and still make money. That is a major change that also went on as a result of all the new participants who came into the marketplace, to encourage size shown on the Street.

Schwartz When you look at a lot of the standard measures of trading costs, we know that commissions have come down. We know that spreads have tightened. A lot of the evidence shows that market impact has come down. Do we all agree on those things? Yes? Okay, get a microphone, we have a "no" over here! So far we are in so much agreement!

---

[12] Black Monday, October 19, 1987. The crash spread from Hong Kong to Europe, hitting the USA after other markets had already declined. The Dow Jones Industrial Average declined by 508 points to 1738.74, or 22.61%.

[13] At the time of writing, International Securities Exchange Holdings, part of Eurex Group, operated two US options exchange, International Securities Exchange (ISE) and ISE Gemini.

[14] See Chapter 2: Opening Address – Equity Market Structure and Regulation: The Last 25 Years. Richard Lindsey, Chief Investment Strategist, Janus Liquid Alternatives.

[Attendee from the floor]: I am from Europe, so unfortunately I will disappoint you a little bit. European market structure is quite different than the US model. The important thing is to discuss for whom we are building these markets, what kind of tools we should be using to satisfy the public. Basically, we have a tool box of different market structure elements.

Schwartz Great point. What I am reading coming out of Europe and here is so much concern about the market structure in Europe. The dimensions of it are, as always, fragmentation and dark pools, and there is a great deal of concern about speed. Maybe I could question the panel more specifically and then get the discussion back to Europe.

First, I would like to address the issue of speed. I see the term "tick size" applied in two ways – one is the price tick, whether it is an eighth or a penny; and the other is a time tick. How fast is the clock ticking? To me the two ticks have interacted. I would like to hear your thoughts about it. At what point is the price tick too small, and at what point is the time tick too fast? Could you give me a millisecond answer?

Pasternak One of the problems is that we opened up the marketplace to your so-called tool box or to different kinds of business models, high-frequency trading, dark pools, price improvement, types of ATSs, internalized order flow, and a variety of other concepts without having a standard. I will give you two examples that are perhaps somewhat controversial. If high-frequency trading only exists for the purpose of having those quotes extracting information, running ahead of the real liquidity seeker, there is no qualitative standard that says, I think we're understanding this. I think we are going to regulate some of these issues. So that is clearly a distraction from market quality, the cost of capital, the willingness to participate, and all the other metrics we use.

On the other hand, regarding internalized order flow – of which I was a big participant in[15] – I could make a case that we were held to a standard of enhanced liquidity, price improvement, continuous quoting of other markets we didn't even create, single price openings, a lot of things, so that if you use quantitative measures of value, I could make a persuasive case. Today the industry still makes a case that it is a free market, that there is enough added value. If you look at the execution metrics and internalized order flow, there is value present there. But the key here is a qualitative analysis of what is happening vis-à-vis market structure, liquidity, and price; and the other part is then letting people innovate.

Harold Bradley I am now an investor. My question is this: Volume is up 10–15 times in the last 15 years, and trading costs for investors (institutions and little guy alike) are down sharply. Does that suggest that market quality is broken? Let's go back to the old days? That is what I am hearing here today.

Sussman Most people agree that most measures of market structure are improved. But US equities as a brand has an image problem. We can cite statistics all day long.

---

[15] This presumably refers to Knight Trading Group of which Pasternak is the former CEO. See footnote 8.

Yet investors haven't come back to the market. When a glitch in the trading of Kraft results in a cover story in *The Wall Street Journal,* because it thinks it is of interest to the public, it means there is an image problem. Why that disconnect? And how does the industry get together to solve that problem? If we just shrug it off, and don't worry, you will not get very far in addressing the issue.

Clark The question earlier was, how fast is too fast? I don't think there is an actual answer. I am going to try the example of the Toronto Stock Exchange that shows you there is a point. The Toronto Stock Exchange is implementing a new trading engine over the next 18 months.[16] It will reduce latency by something on the order of 800 μs. By the time the sound of my voice got to you, more than 800 μs had elapsed! They have said this is due to client demand.

Clients internationally will not trade on the Toronto Stock Exchange unless they reduce their latency by 800 μs. Now 70% of the value traded on the Toronto Stock Exchange on any day is in stocks that are also listed in the USA, either on the NYSE or NASDAQ. Any institutional investor will tell you that, when they give you an order, they expect you to seamlessly make sure they trade in both markets; and so you must give them a single currency fill with a seamless foreign exchange, or FX conversion. For me to send an order to the USA and back at the speed of light takes something like 10 ms. So, if a client gives me an order, my institutional investor expects me to go at 10 ms to the NYSE and back to get that fill.

But the Toronto Stock Exchange will tell you that their institutional investors – so-called clients – will not trade on the TSX because they are 800 ms too slow in execution speed or latency. They, of course, are misusing the word client. A client is somebody who pays them. They are talking about high-frequency traders who at the end of the month get a rebate check. They are actually suppliers. You can call them the suppliers of liquidity, or suppliers of volume, or suppliers of quotes, whatever, but they are not clients. At some point, if my institutional investors – and I am talking about 90-odd percent of them – expect me to represent them in both markets, it must be at an acceptable speed.

Krell I have not seen a definition of high-frequency trading.

Schwartz I was going to ask you that question. You are front running me!

Krell Sorry about that. I wish somebody could please provide one definition. There might be 20 definitions depending on who you ask. My perspective on using computers is to generate a quote. I can tell you that at the ISE we have been doing that since May 26, 2000. That was the day we opened our doors. Why back in 2000? Because we recognized that it was a requirement if you were to provide a marketplace – that is, an automated marketplace – and we were the first one to do that in the options market in the US. To dealers, to market makers, this is essential because we had an average of about 110 different strike prices for every underlying, and quotes for each of those strikes needed to be updated when the underlying moved.

[16] See Don't blink: TMX's new system trades in microseconds. Boyd Erman, *The Globe and Mail.* May 09, 2014.

Now expand that and let's say you are a market maker in 1000 underlyings, meaning you have over 100,000 issues to update. When Microsoft or Apple, or any of the other actives change in price, you have to update all those quotes simultaneously. And the technology has to be in place to process these updates from a variety of different market makers – who all want to update their quotes at the same time. Otherwise their quotes are stale. And if there is a risk of becoming stale, what do they do? They widen their quotes in the first place. They reduce their liquidity.

You want to provide your market makers with the best tools – in order to provide the most efficient marketplace, and in order to have the best quotes in the marketplace with the deepest size. That is the reason why we choose to provide those tools to our dealers. That is a good use of technology.

Now I am not talking, Ken, about the abusive practices that you just pointed out as well. There may be some abusive practices. Still, we shouldn't dismiss the need for using technology to update quotes, just because some people are using those tools in abusive practices. We should root them out. And I will be the first one.

Sussman Good point. Speed bumps aren't going to eliminate abusive trading behavior – they will eliminate one form of abusive trading behavior and someone will just find another form. You really have to go after the trading behaviors that are abusive. If you use technological limitation to prevent abusive trading behavior, you may inadvertently eliminate good trading practices elsewhere. For example, if a really aggressive algo is trying to lift a bunch of quotes in the marketplace, it could potentially result in unintended consequences if a bunch of orders hit the market at the same time as the one experiencing the speed bump.

Schwartz Are you talking about trading being too fast, and are you then asking what we should do about it if we have moved past the optimal point in terms of speed? And when you are talking about speed bumps, how would you go about reconciling this? Are you thinking about some sort of minimum resting period for all stocks or for all orders? That would mean that an order would have to stay in the book, say for a half of a second before it can be pulled?

Sussman Yes. There are different types of speed bumps. You could have a minimum resting period for all stocks, or all orders. You could have a set interval between the exchange matching engine – in other words, anything that would slow down the market. Let's say that having a minimum resting period for all stocks or for all orders is one form of speed bump, or you limit the amount of times you can cancel. It might eliminate some current abusive trading practices. But you would also wind up having a lot of negative impacts on trading practices, and probably generate all sorts of new abuses. You have to go after the things you know are bad – and not necessarily put into place some type of limitation.

Schwartz Will it be beneficial or harmful for the HFT guys, having that minimum half-second resting period?

Sussman I believe it could actually be beneficial. Think about it. When, all of a sudden, everyone who enters the market has to rest their order for some limited amount of time, who are the folks who will be able to respond to that more quickly than anybody else? It would be the HFT participants.

Pasternak You are talking about the same thing. Every one of these suggestions, and David's 800 ms, is all striving to impose a qualitative benefit to the market by imposing a speed bump. David is saying, let's not throw the baby out with the bath water; let innovators in there who are adding to the depth of the market. Let's use technology and regulation. Adam is saying the same thing about adding a half a second or a second – again to try to eliminate those ghost quotes that are extracting information so that they can run ahead.[17]

Sussman Spoofing[18] is already illegal. So what is the problem?

Krell Let's talk about speed. Why is 500 ms the right speed? Where did that come from? Did God come down and say 500 ms, half a second, that's the right number?

[Attendee from the floor]: When I am talking about the tool box and the potential usage of micromarket structures, you have to bring both together in the search for a solution. Then you can use a set of tools. The unfortunate thing is that regulators pick out one single thing that has happened and then try to fix it. You can't really fix something literally. You have to look at the overall strategy. What are you really trying to set up?

Schwartz Do you all agree with that? Sounds pretty intelligent to me. If I can throw my two cents into this. With the properties of the continuous market, trading takes place any time an order to buy matches or crosses an order to sell. You put an order on the book, and how quickly can you get it there, and how quickly someone else can hit it, isn't the main thing. Or, simply put, the difference in time doesn't matter that much. What really matters is who came first, who came second, and who came third. It's like in sporting events, what matters is who won. If it is say, a swim meet where the decorated Olympian, Michael Phelps, is a millisecond ahead of the other guy, Michael Phelps gets the gold. All that matters to Michael Phelps is that he gets there first. By how much does not matter.

With high-speed technology, you can both act in these small fractions of a second and also distinguish who came in first, down to these small fractions of a second.

---

[17] "One criticism relates to its generation of so-called phantom liquidity, in which market liquidity that appears to be provided by HFT may be fleeting and transient due to the posting of and then the almost immediate cancellation of trading orders," according to a summary of concerns of high-frequency trading, referring to "ghost" quotes, popularly known as "phantom" quotes. Source: High-Frequency Trading: Background, Concerns, and Regulatory Developments, Gary Shorter, Rena S. Miller Specialist in Financial Economics, June 19, 2014, *Congressional Research Service*. http://fas.org/sgp/crs/misc/R43608.pdf

[18] Ibid. FINRA, the frontline broker dealer regulator, has observed that "although many HFT strategies are legitimate, some are not and may be used for manipulative purposes [and] given the scale of the potential impact these practices may have, the surveillance of abusive algorithms remains a high priority for FINRA…. [A]reas of concern [include] … the use of so-called 'momentum ignition strategies' where a market participant attempts to induce others to trade at artificially high or low prices. Examples of this activity reportedly include layering and spoofing strategies."

But the technology does not change the reality that somebody came first, somebody second, and somebody third. Does the speed acceleration attributable to technology have negative impacts? In my work with my doctoral student Nazli Sila Alan,[19] we have looked at volatility over very short periods of time. On the NYSE, we have observed that the volatility has gone up. On NASDAQ, it has sort of fluctuated around, but has trended neither up nor down. But at the NYSE it has gone up. Is that because of speed? Is it because of fragmentation? What is causing this? Is volatility another metric that we should be looking at? I suggest that it is.

What is gained economically from actions taking place in a second, a half a second, or these little milliseconds? I know that we are all impatient to get results.

I can understand the impatience. But impatience down to a sub-second? Can you tell me what we really gain, and what we might lose? Adam, can I ask you? You have been into these statistics.

Sussman Speed is a reflection of fundamentals we try to instill in markets. You know that is true when you go back to what once made our markets slower – and was the issue regulators set out to solve.[20] It was certainty of execution and transparency. Faster execution speeds is a consequence of trying to facilitate those features. So to say, look at what we gained as a result of speed is one thing. But I would kind of reverse it and say that speed is the result of more transparency and certainty of execution that we have in the marketplace today. Now maybe not everyone values those things as much as others do. Maybe the HFTs have benefited from speed more than other participants.

Schwartz I can see "faster" being a great benefit if you are going from minutes to seconds. But as you go from seconds to microseconds, when is enough enough?

Pasternak Bob, we are misunderstanding something here. Doug had a Freudian slip when he described the people who were demanding speed changes in Toronto?

Clark I actually said they were not clients of the Toronto Stock Exchange because the Toronto Stock Exchange is paying them. In economic reality, when I am paying you, I am not your client.

Pasternak The real distinction here would occur if you told an investor they are going to give up speed, but then have a greater degree of confidence as a result. You, the investor, are going to get better prices and better liquidity. You would trade every day. I am not talking about high-frequency traders, day traders, or even short-term traders. And we are losing that distinction here. Frankly, there are too many innovators who have models that are really focused on speed.

---

[19] Fairfield University.

[20] This is a reference to the "price manipulation" charges against NASDAQ market markers which regulators set out to address with the introduction of the Order Handling Rules in 1997. Prior to the Order Handling Rules, NASDAQ was a less automated marketplace where order execution speeds were slower overall than today.

Sussman Don't you agree that it would seem that the better solution is to rewrite some of the regulations, not to write more regulations? We have to undo some of the things that created this market, not necessarily say, "Oh you know what the solution is, let's put a 500 ms speed bump in." I don't think that will get you what you want as an investor.

Pasternak I don't know what the solution is because I am not that involved in the actual mechanics in the marketplace today, the exception being in regard to a $100 million dollar equities fund I run as an investor. As Harold says, I am deeply interested. But as one of the innovators today, I would say that is behind me. I am 58, so speaking as an investor, the conversation has to be changed. I don't know what the solution is. Is it imposing qualitative standards? Is it part of what you're saying? My guess is that it is all of the above. The conversation needs to be moved a bit to market quality, away from particular instances of either a computer glitch like Knight's example, the Kraft example, or these 10 ms conversations – and into a much broader conversation about how to improve the markets again around liquidity and price.

Clark When you are talking about reducing execution speeds by milliseconds or microseconds, what you are typically taking out are the safety checks. Certainty of execution is great. But if certainty of execution comes at a cost of systemic risk in a marketplace, it is just not worth it.

Krell Great point, Doug. I agree with you. I can say no one has perfect systems. Let's all agree to that. Every system will fail at some point. The question on the table is how do we mitigate those issues? How do we control them? How do we make sure they don't become systemic? How do we prevent catastrophes from happening? Ken, what happened at Knight on August 1, was it a catastrophe?

By the way, that was not a high-frequency occurrence. That was a surge in volume. So it is not just price controls. It is also volume controls. It is the surge of how much activity comes into the marketplace that can be absorbed in whatever time slice you want to take. That is what we should all concentrate on – controls.

Wayne Arden [Arden Consulting] I used to work for NASDAQ OMX for many years. David was also one of my customers. It would be a very dangerous road to take if the government was the regulator, and the Securities and Exchange Commission, or the Commodity Futures Trading Commission, was then to artificially limit technology. You have examples on this panel of successful entrepreneurs who have used technology to make very positive differences in the USA. The ISE, for example, through innovative technology in 2000, through a savvy management team, and through nuances in market structure, became one of the leading options exchanges in the country in a relatively short period of time. If the government were to say that we should limit high-frequency trading to a delay of a millisecond or 10 ms, that could over time weaken the US markets.

There is another approach. If you think about most of the US equities markets, they don't charge fees for orders, only for executed trades. If you go back about 15 or 20 years ago, that wasn't much of a big deal because the ratio of orders to trades was maybe 3 to 1. Now the ratio is 100 to 1 at some exchange. The retail investor, to an extent, is subsidizing high-frequency trading. It would be a better approach by the regulators to consider charging for orders. So there is clearly economic value. Speaking as a technologist, an exchange has to spend a lot of money to support the marketplace. There are a lot of routers, high-speed networks, servers, and so on. If that is the business strategy of an exchange, being able to support that costs money.

If the industry were to charge for orders in addition to trades, that would not limit technology – and it would also make the system more fair. Some high-frequency traders would not survive that transition, but others could.

Clark There are a couple of countries in the world, including Canada, that have actually gone that route this year. Canada implemented the Integrated Fee Model on April 1 this year.[21] But they have done it very carefully. They believe that technology cost is driven by the number of orders. So they divvy that out to the various brokers, or participants, based on their market share in message traffic. It is not a new fee, it is not a new tax like the French Financial Transaction Tax.[22] It is just a reallocation of an existing cost.

This fee model works very well in Canada.[23] Its order to trade ratio on April 1 was about 75 orders per fill; it is now down to 50. It has seen about a 17.5% decrease in the number of messages across the market. There has also been a decrease in volume, but that is in line with the rest of the world. I like that. I am not in favor of some new tax that is just another tax on the industry. But I don't mind a reallocation of fees to correctly charge those who are causing the cost. I don't mind that at all.

Brett Redfearn [JP Morgan, from the floor.] Speed is something that enables market makers to manage risk. Information is moving faster today than ever before. And the ability to get in quickly is a key part of the ability to manage risk and provide liquidity. So that would be a plus in terms of speed. A negative would potentially be part of the compensation model, and in terms of latency arbitrage. If some participants are faster than everybody else, then they can essentially trade in some markets and trade opportunistically relative to other venues, given some of the latency.

That said, my questions here should help frame our understanding: What is the market maker model today? How are market makers compensated? When we think about slowing down the market, there are multiple types of high-frequency traders that need to be taken into consideration, and this gets back to the importance of defining HFT. For example, there are participants that are providers of liquidity, that

[21] The Investment Industry Regulatory Organization of Canada (IIROC) introduced the Integrated Fee Model on April 1, 2012, encompassing a fee structure to recover market regulatory costs. The structure is based on the message traffic and trading activity of participants in a way that allocates IIROC's annual operating cost to two pools, comprising distinct costs for dealer regulation and market regulation.

[22] This French Financial Transaction Tax on the purchase of certain French equities was adopted by the French parliament and was enacted August 1, 2012.

[23] See 21.

is to say, providers posting non-marketable limit orders; and then there are takers of liquidity, primarily using marketable orders. Providers are often market makers; takers are more likely to be engaged in statistical arbitrage. If we slowed down the market, we would then introduce new challenges to the market makers, or providers of liquidity. And that's while creating new advantages for the takers, who would have an easier time picking off the market maker quotes that have to post, or remain accessible in the market, for a longer period of time – while the rest of the data in the market is still being disseminated at light speed.

I would ask your thoughts about David's earlier point on maker-taker. One could argue that the rebates for makers and the fees for takers, which are largely set by the mandated fee cap under Reg NMS,[24] are unnecessarily high, creating a misallocation of liquidity in the market. The uniform fee structure inevitably results in the same market maker compensation formula, regardless of whether a stock is extremely liquid or extremely illiquid. This has also resulted in an oversupply of liquidity for naturally liquid securities and an undersupply of liquidity for less liquid securities. So we need to ask whether the maker-taker pricing structure and, in particular, the access fee cap might be tweakable at some point. In other words, should a modified rebate-fee approach take into consideration the differing characteristics of different securities? I would argue that the rebates (and fees) are too high for active names, while the compensation model for illiquid stocks is inadequate.

I'd like to make another point that addresses the issue of quote accessibility which was a fundamental objective of Reg NMS. With Reg NMS, our markets – specifically the NYSE – were basically mandated to be fast, and quotes had to be automatically accessible if they were to be "protected." So we evolved to a fast, automated market structure to ensure that quotes would be accessible. But in the arms race for speed, have we gone too far? Have we become too fast?

I ask this because, in today's marketplace, quotes can be canceled in microseconds, sometimes even faster than a market participant can access a displayed quote. If trading speeds are so fast that an "automated" quote can be canceled before it can be physically accessed, have we solved the challenge of quote accessibility?

Krell Brett, you are right. And Doug talked about this before: It is the complexity of the entire fee structure on all the exchanges, not just the equity exchanges, but on the options exchanges as well. Complexity is at a new high in this regard.

I am sure that, at JP Morgan, you have a team that is analyzing every change that is taking place. And change is occurring almost daily. We have to monitor what our competitors are doing, and we are trying to do the best that we can. We tweak our fee structure on an almost regular basis. We have to do that to stay competitive. It is not just the market maker-taker side – that is just one facet of it. The fee structure has become very competitive. Andy, by the way, we now have ten options markets.

---

[24] Regulation National Market System (NMS) was enacted by the Securities and Exchange Commission in 2007 to foster competition among US exchanges and individual orders and to promote fairness in price executions across all exchanges and platforms.

Sussman Is that it? You have a long way to go to catch up to the US equities. Good luck!

Krell Well, exchanges.

Sussman Oh, okay.

Schwartz Three more are needed to catch up! [laughter]

Sussman Good technology is supposed to take complex processes and simplify them. We haven't seen the benefit of that in US equities market in terms of the cost and the complexity. To the contrary, the cost and the availability of technology have made things more complex than they should be. But we actually got there in part because of the regulatory sandbox in which everybody is forced to play. Do we have to go back and revisit a lot of the regulations that got us here in light of the technologies of today?

Anthony Fortunato [Instinet] David, you just mentioned fees and the changing of fees. I wonder if you could elaborate a little further. Perhaps Adam could also jump in. When a stock or options exchange changes a fee, is it targeting one, two, or three large participants? It seems that since the exchanges have to treat everybody equally, it sets hurdles that clearly only one, two, or three people can clear. In doing so, that is how the liquidity moves from exchange A to exchange B. Is that fair? Is that part of the problem? Or is that just a reality you have to deal with?

Sussman It just happens, even going back to when I was at Datek. If we had a problem we couldn't solve ourselves, we would go to Island, our sister ECN, and say, "Hey, we are trying to accomplish this, can you help us?" Sure enough, Island would build the order type for Datek, because they would know what to do. So they initially built it for us, and then over time they would roll it out to the rest of our clients.

I think that still happens today. Brokers will often approach a trading venue (say an exchange or dark pool) with the same idea in mind. They want to interact with that venue and inform that venue that it might make more sense for it to create an order type that fits its parameters, rather than having the broker program that into its own infrastructure. Generally speaking, it transpires that way. In other words, a large participant would say, "Hey, we want to implement this new strategy, we could do it on our side, but it probably makes a lot more sense to do it on your side."

Fortunato You are talking about order types. I was specifically talking about fee structures. It seems like the fee structures are a lot different.

Sussman Yes. It is a similar situation in that a particular strategy would work better based on a fee structure.

Krell There is segmentation going on. You see that to some extent by the proliferation of exchanges. The NYSE now has more than one options market. NASDAQ has more than one options market. Why? CBOE has more than one options market. Why? Because they are targeting different segments and are providing order types as well as a fee structure, for a specific targeted audience in that marketplace.

We have submitted a filing for a second market at ISE for the same reason. So there is segmentation happening.

Schwartz I would tantalizingly like to wrap it up with a question. We have been focusing on the quality of markets. How has it changed? In the 15 years since the Order Handling Rules were introduced, there has been a tremendous amount of technological change. And technology changes the game, and, as it does, it also calls for rethinking regulation. Does regulation keep up with it? We have a panel coming up shortly that will address that. In today's environment, it really does boil down to speed and tick sizes and things like that. At what point is small too small, at what point is fast too fast?

Adam, you talked about transparency and it made me wonder – with this really high-speed stuff, I can't even see that fast? But you can't operate that quickly, unless you are armed with algorithms that have been computerized. So you have computers talking to computers. We used to have our computers handling orders and routing information. Then we had computers making trades. Now we have computers generating orders. As that happens, computers are talking to computers. That is a seismic change. What sort of environment are we moving into? How do we deal with it? I hope we keep circling around questions such as this as our day progresses. It is terribly important. If the answer is that real fast is too fast, what should we do about it?

These are very, very tough questions. What does this all imply about market quality in general, and about price discovery in particular? Are we doing a better job now? Are we still having trouble finding the right price to trade at? Can you say yes or no to this?

Clark I am going to take 25 s to tell a really quick story.

Schwartz No, take 2 s. Take a microsecond. No, go on Doug, I am sorry. [laughter]

Clark My brother-in-law lives in Toronto. He does a lot of consulting here in the US. He was paid recently by a firm. He then had US $150,000 that he wanted to convert into Canadian dollars. He said to me, how can I do that? He went to his bank and told them that he wanted to convert this sum into Canadian dollars. They said they were going to charge him a fee of 2% for the transaction. He came back to me and said, you got to be able to do better for me. I called up my bank, and they offered to do it for 1%. I used to run this bank's program trading desk, so I called its head of FX trading. He said that I can get it done for about three tenths of 1%, or actually 35 pips. And my brother-in-law said that is fantastic. I had just reduced his cost tremendously.

However, I said we are not doing that trade, Dave. Here is what we did. We bought 1873 shares of TD Bank on the NYSE or in the US market. We actually did it in a variety of venues and dark pools. And a second later we sold that same stock back in Canada – and we did that trade for 32 pips instead of 35. The equity markets work. We made better price discovery on our trades then we do on FX, or in fixed income. That was two trades, not one trade. Two commissions, the all-in cost was 90% lower than the best price that I could have gotten.

Schwartz Price discovery for the underlyings, for the equities, is very important for you, David. How do you feel about it? Good or bad?

Krell Good. We think of it as Richard said in his opening remarks – the markets have never been more efficient, they have never been less expensive to operate in, and they have never been deeper when you really need the liquidity.

Schwartz I love to have optimists on the panel. Ken?

Pasternak To harken on this innovation process and free marketplace is a conversation about continually improving things. We have to keep a lot of the imperfections in perspective. We have a great marketplace, but we can get an even better marketplace.

Schwartz I like that last point, we can get better.

Sussman While we are patting ourselves on the back for all of this improvement, the naysayers – the critics of the high-frequency markets – are controlling the narrative. We can't let go of that fact. We need to focus on it, instead of just citing statistics to a room full of people who already believe in it. How are we going to go out and tell that story? All of us who support today's markets have a collective interest in doing that.

Schwartz Good point to ponder as we conclude. I would like to give these guys a big round of applause. Thank you.

Chapter 3
Competition, Incentives, and Innovations in the Great American Marketplace

Frank Hatheway

Robert Schwartz It is with great pleasure I introduce my professional colleague and long-time friend, Frank Hatheway. In doing so, I would like to share a story with you about Frank. As many of you already know, I have been a proponent of call auctions for many years. In my efforts to build support, I had talked to Frank and NASDAQ in the past about introducing a call auction at NASDAQ. I did not meet with a great deal of success. Well, lo and behold, one day I was in my office at Baruch at about 5:30 in the afternoon when my phone rang. "Hello, Bob, it's Frank," the voice on the other end said. "We are doing it Bob. We are putting in a call!"

Frank started to utter the word "auction" when the fire alarm suddenly went off in my building and it cut Frank off in mid-sentence. Can you imagine? All of these years of waiting and, just as Frank calls, the fire alarm goes off! I was shouting, "Frank, Frank," and then this other voice comes over the intercom, saying, "This is not a drill, you need to vacate the building!" Afterward, I learned that the fire alarm was set off because a professor on the tenth floor had suddenly overheated! [Laughter]

Frank and I picked up our conversation the next day. He said, "Yes, NASDAQ is introducing a call auction," and was I ever pleased. Please welcome Frank Hatheway.

Frank Hatheway I was once a trader. I then became an academic, and now I am back doing industry things. I am, fundamentally, an economist. It is said that to every carpenter everything looks like a nail. Of course, I don't use a hammer in my job despite what some of my staff might think about my management style. But my figurative hammer, as I look at market structure issues, is the role of incentives. Every time I see something that is transformative, or that is resisting change, I ask what are the incentives? So my talk is essentially organized around incentives. In an industry where the suggestion that one should follow the money is often sound advice, I think that organizing and structuring this talk around incentives is a reasonable thing to do.

F. Hatheway (✉)
NASDAQ OMX Group, Inc., New York, NY, USA

R.A. Schwartz et al. (eds.), *Rapidly Changing Securities Markets*,
Zicklin School of Business Financial Markets Series,
DOI 10.1007/978-3-319-54588-2_3

I will focus on the US model and will try, at least in my formal remarks, to stay clear of specific detail. I will focus on the role of our industry which is essentially about a couple of things. It is about transforming current savings into future consumption. It is to enable investments in businesses which reward the entrepreneur, the investor, and the employee as well. At this point, I don't think anybody doubts that I am an economist when I use words like that.

I define an initiator in a very simple and high-level way. They are those who do not benefit from the status quo, either directly or indirectly. I break down initiators into revolutionaries and marginalists. Typically, you view an initiator as someone who is in the business in some way, shape, or form, either currently or potentially. But they could also be regulators.

I further break down initiators into revolutionaries and marginalists. As we'll discuss, these terms are not normative. Both types of initiators are extremely important and here's an example from our industry. A revolutionary is someone like Jerome Pustilnik and Herbert Behrens who founded the Institutional Networks Corporation in 1967. A marginalist would be someone like Bill Lupien, who took that company and made it into Instinet. All three are initiators.[1] I consider Pustilnik and Behrens revolutionaries because they launched electronic trading in US cash equities. I consider Lupien the marginalist because, under him, Instinet realized the full potential of what Pustilnik and Behrens had created. As I said, this distinction isn't normative and both revolutionaries and marginalists are very important as initiators.

I am also introducing a different type of actor that is not really in the title of this conference – I call this actor a catalyzer. There are different types of catalyzers, the people who make things happen. There are pure catalyzers. There are catalyzers who could be initiators but who have chosen for one reason or another to try and spur others to action rather than creating initiatives themselves. Typical of this latter group are the press, politicians, and regulators. Behind the catalyzers are a large number of people, a large number of potential agents who drive the catalyzers.

There are temporal aspects that are necessary for initiators to accomplish their goals. In economic terminology, in the long term, we can essentially change everything. We can change the capital we apply to an issue. We can change the methods of production. We can change the needs and wants that motivate consumers. In the long run, everything is up in the air.

I will look at the temporal dimension more from a political or even sociological viewpoint. This viewpoint focuses on the emergence of consensus among the various constituents that are in any industry, including ours. I will talk about the need for

[1] Instinet was founded by Jerome M. Pustilnik and Herbert R. Behrens and incorporated in 1967 as Institutional Networks Corp. Instinet was set up to compete with the New York Stock Exchange, bypassing specialists through a system of computer links between major institutions. By December 1969, Instinet was activated and became a game changer in buying and selling equity securities in an automated, anonymous, and confidential basis.

The pickup rate remained slow until 1983, when Instinet recruited William A. "Bill" Lupien, a former Pacific Stock Exchange specialist, to run the company. Lupien embarked on a successful campaign to market the system more aggressively to the broker community, rather than focusing exclusively on the buy-side as previously done.

convergence, an agreement that change is necessary, and that a specific proposed change may be appropriate. Maybe that change happens; maybe it doesn't. Finally, I will devote the last few minutes of my remarks to things in the current US model that perhaps might be where we would see initiators act differently.

I'll begin by saying that an initiator does not benefit from the status quo. They can come from many different aspects of the private sector. In certain circumstances, I would include regulators in that category. As I said, initiators can be marginalists or revolutionaries. A marginalist is someone who is essentially struggling over reallocating the status quo. A revolutionary is outside the status quo and wants to reform how it is done. We had some revolutionaries on the panel this morning. Innovation typically occurs when you have a combination of both. That is in part because there are tremendous fixed costs in any business that need to change. In this industry, where capital has been allocated, savings have been converted into future consumption through the investment process over a long period. Initiatives tend to be a combination of revolution and marginalism.

I know it is simplistic to say that initiators may be those who do not benefit from the status quo. I want to refine that idea through this distinction between not benefiting directly as opposed to not benefiting indirectly. There are those who do not directly benefit from the status quo because they essentially pay for something that is part of the status quo; but that doesn't provide the benefits associated with the costs. The costs can fall into two broad dimensions: economic rents and substandard product offerings. Economic rents in this context mean excess costs for investors and excess profits for intermediaries. We talked again this morning about how the costs of trading, direct and indirect, have declined. There may have been rents in trading costs in the past. There probably were rents in trading activities toward the end of the manual trading environment in the USA, albeit telephone or floor based. People also can pay through substandard products and services. Both dimensions are standard competition theory; in other words, I am not getting what I paid for, I am paying too much.

When we talk about economic rents, remember this: established businesses that are able to extract rents and are paid a handsome rate of return on what they produce are also those businesses that encourage innovation and attract talent. They can be okay things to have at least for the short run. But established businesses are also prone to extract economic rents if they are not constrained. The ideal constraint, again from the economist's point of view, is competition. If you don't have competition, and someone is extracting rents where there is no competition, you don't have innovation. You essentially have a tax. You have a formal or informal tax. One of the themes in my talk is the role of government. What we have, what we have evolved from, and what we may evolve into.

When we think about people who do not directly benefit – and tie into some other things that I have mentioned at the beginning – these folks tend to be marginalists. They are already in the industry. So the situation tends to be that I am paying someone else too much for something I already buy; or I am getting poor service for what I pay. A marginalist thinks, 'Let's change what's going on.' I want to be an initiator and change the world. But because these folks tend to be in the industry, they don't want to upset the status quo too much. As a marginalist, I opened this nice business; I would like a bigger piece of it. But I don't necessarily want the whole business to transform itself in terms of how it is done, because I personally have invested in skills, in relationships, etc., in order to make this business work. I also may have invested in employees, in physical plans, and in other things that I do not want to change.

Those who do not benefit from the status quo, and are our indirect participants, can be both marginalists in my mind and revolutionaries. Indirectly, they bare the excessive fees, or the lousy services get passed through to them. They also incur costs because of a lack of innovation. They aren't offered new and more efficient products and services. There could also be a cost to individuals from the status quo (and for regulators and other people into this.) The status quo could also be a threat to their own position, to their own careers, to those of the institution they represent.

Status quo is something that would potentially make them a target of criticism for not doing their job. This class tends to be the slowest to mobilize. They have less skin in the game than some of the direct participants have. But when they do mobilize, they are more adept at driving revolutionary rather than marginal change. That is because they have less to gain by simply tweaking or redividing the current pot.

The role of catalyzers belongs in a conference with a theme like today's, not just because it is the 15th anniversary of the Order Handling Rules[2] but in large part because catalyzers are very active right now around market structure in the USA and in Europe. Catalyzers, as I said at the beginning, include the press, politicians, and self-appointed activists who go in search of an issue. Regulators, the press, and politicians are what I would call pure catalyzers, actors who are not positioned to be initiators and who chose to stay that way. Their skills and institutional constraints are not structured that way.

Who drives the catalyzer? It goes back to some of the questions that were raised today. It tends to be the end consumer. These are people that when you think about a catalyzer considering a very broad range of constituencies, a very broad possible set of issues, you ask, why are they talking about our issues? Because people are interested in our issues. In the equities world, the driver of the catalyzers is the investor, either indirect retail investors through institutions or else direct retail investors themselves. It can also be entrepreneurs, people who want capital to build their businesses. In the current environment in the USA and Europe, it can be workers, people who want jobs. They don't know how what we do or what NASDAQ OMX does running an exchange, or what the rest of you in this room do running your businesses, but they want jobs.

---

[2] The Order Handling Rules were introduced by the Securities and Exchange Commission in 1997. The Limit Order Display and the Quote Rules, enacted as part of the regulation, paved the way for today's "modern" high-speed electronic markets, starting with the early wave of upstart Electronic Communications Networks or ECNs. See Securities and Exchange Commission, Order Execution Obligation, http://www.sec.gov/rules/final/37619a.txt

Regarding the press as a catalyzer, I want to distinguish between press activities and reports about business successes and failures. The latter always go on. Reports about market ups and downs, those always go on. What I am focusing on is the press stories about how the markets work. This is what Adam Sussman of Aite Group was talking about earlier at this conference today when he was referring to image issues. In my view, most of these stories wouldn't exist if we do what we are supposed to do. If we operate in a way that people have no concerns about.

I remember the first story I ever read about market structure, a very long time ago. My initial job was working as an engineer for General Electric (GE). General Electric's employee magazine ran a story about the GE specialist. Some silver-haired gentleman had a book in his hand when he had his picture snapped at the New York Stock Exchange (NYSE) – he was the guy who kept General Electric shares trading in a fair and orderly manner. That was my introduction to market structure; that was my image. Many of us have visited with NASDAQ market makers. Kenny Pasternak's firm[3] was generous in letting us see how the sausage was made in the manual days of trading. I also spent time with a floor governor, Bob Seijus. Other people from the NYSE were very generous with their time and were charming people. Either through the press or via direct experience, you could relate to professional traders of the past.

Today, you can't have a cup of coffee anywhere near our servers at NASDAQ, and anyway, it is really not a whole lot of fun hanging out with our servers! You don't learn much from spending time with our servers. Right now, we don't really need people to understand what happens when money goes into the market and flows into this trading machine. Some people may understand the process, but many don't. And so we say, "Trust us." But we don't have a mechanism that makes it easy for individuals to trust us. We also don't have a mechanism right now where representatives of the public can have an easy time understanding how the market works.

So we are attracting a lot of interest from the press. The stories are global, there are many conferences about market structure, and politicians are very interested in market structure. To me, that is evidence of the powerful role the catalyzer plays today. And the politicians are also initiators.

I assume that not too many of us here went through the adoption of the National Market System Amendments in 1975.[4] I wasn't trading then, I am not that old! I was at least thinking about what my first job would be back then. The Commodities

[3] In 1995, Pasternak cofounded Knight Trading Group in 1995 along with Walter Raquet. Pasternak served as the company's CEO from 1995 until he retired on January 21, 2002. At the time of writing, Pasternak was the founder and executive chairman of The KABR Group and also managing principal of Chestnut Ridge Capital. Pasternak, chairman of affiliate, KABR Real Estate, was a panelist at this same conference. See chapter Fifteen Years After the Order Handling Rules, How Do the Markets Look Today?

[4] Federal legislation launched on June 4, 1975, to amend the Securities Exchange Act of 1934. The 1975 amendments instructed the Securities and Exchange Commission to cooperate with the industry in creating a national market system and laid the groundwork for the clearance and settlement of securities transactions nationwide. The amendments also mandated the prohibition of fixed-commission rates, promulgated earlier by the Securities and Exchange Commission in its Rule 19b-3.

Futures Modernization Act in 2000,[5] yes, that was certainly enacted during the career of many of us in this room. Obviously politicians' engagement in this industry goes way back to The Securities Act and the Exchange Act of 1933 and 1934.[6] Think of the political segment as a catalyzer – they tend to be unpredictable. You don't know exactly what they are going to do. But you will have to live with it. So we have them.

Let's now move on to some other points, the temporal issues. In the area of initiators, we do have very, very capable people inside and outside this industry who might like to change how it operates. There is a lot of money around, and that always attracts interest. If we have catalyzers – and we do right now around the issue of how the markets work – then why doesn't change just occur? The short answer is the power of incumbency, the power of the status quo. Status quo is always hard to change. The economic view of the long term is the time it takes to change installed capital. Installed capital is the invested capital that we all have a stake in, maybe at sunk costs.

You probably took an MBA and heard of sunk costs. You should ignore them, but people don't. It takes time to change the habits of producers, how we do things. It takes time to change the habits of consumers. Installing physical capital is expensive; acquiring human capital with the appropriate skills takes time. And there is also (as I said) the political and sociological view. It takes time to get consensus. People are invested in the status quo. Sometimes literally, sometimes psychologically, and sometimes both.

Change will be resisted until it is forced or a consensus is achieved. Initiators are successful when there is convergence. There must be a need for change that is acknowledged and accepted. Then you must have a consensus of how change would be accomplished and at least some degree of agreement on the appropriateness of this change.

The Order Handling Rules of 1997 started all the ongoing changes in the way security markets work. There was a short-run vision of how the markets would work following the Order Handling Rules. There were longer-run visions in some people's minds about what would ultimately happen. But there wasn't a long-run vision in the sense of everything actually changing. Great big buildings at Broad and Wall Street in New York City[7] are being used in different ways today. Whole professions cease to exist. What would that world look like? That is what we are talking about now.

---

[5] US federal legislation of over-the-counter (OTC) derivatives signed into law by President Bill Clinton in December 2000. The law required that most OTC derivatives transactions between "sophisticated parties" would not be regulated as "futures" under the Commodity Exchange Act of 1936 (CEA), or as "securities" under the federal securities laws. The major dealers of these products would have their dealings in OTC derivatives continued to be supervised by their federal regulators under general principles of "safety and soundness." Most importantly, the Act permitted the trading of single stock futures.

[6] The Securities Act of 1933, federal legislation on the sale of securities, was enacted following the market crash of 1929. Before this, regulation of securities was mostly overseen by state laws. The Securities Act of 1934 established the Securities and Exchange Commission.

[7] Refers to the New York Stock Exchange in lower Manhattan.

Where might we see innovation, who might be the innovators, where are they going to come from? I will start off with who is potentially an initiator. It is anyone who has to buy or sell a product or service which is somehow encumbered in regulatory, legal, or standardized business practices that limit consumers from getting what they want: getting an innovative, effective product or service at a low cost. The people behind the Institutional Networks Corp./Instinet were initiators because they thought market structure in the 1960s kept institutions from trading in a manner that was best for them.

One of the reasons encumbrances arise is that a lot of the services of our industry are governed by economies of scale. Scale, in and of itself, creates resistance to innovation. In principle, when you think about initiators, they could be brokers, investment advisers, exchanges, or clearing houses. Their customers represent investors, advise investors, and are investors themselves and purchasers of exchange services – essentially almost anyone in the industry would be on your list of marginalists. In terms of how we normally think of the industry, I would also add technologists.

In the old days, Bill Donaldson[8] broke the model of what it took to be a broker. He was a broker. Most of the firms on the Street today have replaced a great many of their brokers. To hear the firms tell it, they replaced a great many of their brokers with a great many technologists who actually are paid more than the brokers. These technology folks know today's business.

The catalysts, who we already talked about, are actively promoting change. So where might we see innovation? Where would the initiators be coming from today? Is it a start-up? Or, in keeping with a central theme of these conferences, will it be the exchange space, will it be market structures, and would it be the listings themselves?

The intensity of direct innovation and competition around trade executions has been vibrant for a number of years, particularly for the most widely traded stocks. But there is certainly dissatisfaction among the catalyzers. You heard that this morning in the questions and in some of the comments from the panel. Less vocally, initiators aren't necessarily happy. There is a particular emphasis on the way the US markets operate, and we got a taste of that this morning.

There is also a global view that whatever non-US regulators might do, they should make certain that (name your jurisdiction) the non-US jurisdictions' market structure does not look like the US version. Maybe that is a valid view; maybe that is not. Maybe what we are doing with market structure is an idea like representative democracy that will prove itself in time. Maybe it is like Prohibition[9] that will not be viewed so favorably by the judgment of time.

---

[8] William (Bill) Donaldson, cofounder of Donaldson, Lufkin & Jenrette, and chairman and CEO of the New York Stock Exchange from 1990 to 1995, was Chairman of the Securities and Exchange Commission from 2003 until 2005.

[9] In the USA, "Prohibition" is remembered for the nationwide ban and restrictions on the transportation, import, export, and sale of alcoholic beverages from January 1920 through 1933. The ban aimed to moderate social behavior and curb crime and corruption. However, backroom dealing in the distribution of alcohol flourished along with organized crime.

How about marginal change? Let's do things simply and work up to something a little more complex. For example, trading continues to evolve in the direction of linked pools operated mostly by brokers. Initiators of continuing this change will be the brokers themselves, to a lesser extent technologists. Exchanges are probably not so much initiators in the world. Regulators also need to be initiators, or at least they should change the way they do things because such a structure of linked pools in many ways is reminiscent of the way the old NASDAQ operated in the early 1990s.

The regulators were not altogether happy with the way NASDAQ operated in the early 1990s. If the market evolves in the direction of linked dealer pools through marginal change, the regulators need to decide whether perhaps a market like the old NASDAQ is the way to go. Or they may decide that there are some rules from the old NASDAQ that they don't want to put in place again, perhaps the Order Handling Rules from 1997. Because these rules are not really the way we wanted to go – and we need not repeat that.

Another marginal change – and this would be one that makes me happier since I'm speaking for an exchange – is an evolution that reconsolidates trading. It could happen. It may happen by originating, so to speak, in the less active of securities. Such a change may initiate more from the dealer community than broker dealers per se. Certainly, exchanges and people that operate exchange-like entities such as ECNs (to use the US term) and, again, regulators have to be initiators.

The revolution and revolutionary change – and one that has often been promised but has not delivered – would be an eBay style of trading with far less of a role for intermediaries than today. Most of us in this room don't work in an eBay-style world. The role of the broker clearly changes. Obviously, an initiative like this would have to come largely from the technology side and the regulator, because it would disrupt so many business models. Our friends at the DTCC and NSCC[10] would have to change what they do. All the credit issues, and all the various issues that go along with the broker-client relationship, will cease to be relevant. The broker, if anything, becomes more of a banker or technology provider – and focuses less on many of the activities the broker carries out today.

On the listing side, does the JOBS Act[11] serve as a catalyst for revolutionary change? The JOBS Act came from the political process, not from a securities industry body or from exchanges or the SEC. It was driven by firms dissatisfied with the capital formation process, and it came up quickly. How well it was thought through is subject to debate. It certainly didn't cover everything that is necessary for a complete liberalization of listing and trading processes. But, to me, it reflects

[10] The Depository Trust & Clearing Corporation (DTCC) is the US post-trade financial services company facilitating clearing and settlement services to the financial markets. It also provides central custody of securities. DTCC was established in 1999 as a holding company to combine the Depository Trust Company (DTC) and the National Securities Clearing Corporation (NSCC) in the automated clearing and settlement of securities.

[11] The Jumpstart Our Business Startups (JOBS) Act was signed into law by President Barack Obama in April 5, 2012. It was designed to assist small private business in raising money so that they could expand and hire workers.

something a bit more fundamental. Private equity has grown, and it has grown a lot – and it is big. It is not as big as public equity, but it is big.

So here is a question the JOBS Act provides: Do we want two structures for investment, one public and one private? If we want one, or essentially one, which should we move toward? Should public equity look more like private equity? Or should private equity look more like public equity? The JOBS Act is a step toward answering those questions.

Other businesses on the exchange side are also probably right for innovation. When Regulation ATS[12] and then Regulation NMS[13] were both put in place, it created the potential for broker dealers to sell market data. Right now, only exchanges and self-regulatory organizations, or SROs, can sell market data. There is no particular reason it has to be that way.

Where else should we think about initiators coming from? In many ways, that is hard to answer because it is part of the status quo that we accept. Maybe not all of us accept it all of the time, but it is generally something we view as needing to change. You think of major initiatives, and that is where revolutionary change should come from. When thinking about what you are going to change, one starting point that is somewhat simpler to deal with is thinking about what is old. It has been the way it is for a long time – and we tweak around the edges to make it run a little better.

For example, the clearing and settlement process in the USA is old. The three clearing houses came together in the 1970s. They introduced some major revisions in clearing and settlement to solve a paperwork crisis where we had to shut trading down every Wednesday afternoon. Essentially, that structure, established in the 1970s, is more or less what we follow today.

Lots of change is coming on the over-the-counter derivatives side. Will there be spillover on the other side into what we do in the equity markets? What happens to everybody's role in this industry? What happens to how we do things in clearing and settlement? Will there be changes, like I mentioned a couple minutes ago, to make the markets more eBay-like?

How about initiators on the regulatory side? We have had the current regulatory structure for a long time. Commissioner Gallagher[14] was talking earlier in the week about exchange models and ATS models. You may not have thought through exactly what converging the exchange and broker dealer ATS models means. But that would be a big change.

---

[12] See RIN 3235-AH41

Regulation of Exchanges and Alternative Trading Systems, https://www.sec.gov/rules/final/34-40760.txt Release No. 34-40760; File No. S7-12-98.

[13] Reg NMS (Regulation National Market System) was adopted by the Securities and Exchange Commission in 2005 and introduced 2 years later to further advance the ideals of a national market system. The regulation includes the order protection or trade-through rule; access rule (fair access) to market data including quotations; rules on sub-penny trading and on market data.

[14] Daniel Gallagher, Securities and Exchange Commissioner.

Another view for possible regulatory change would be changing from an approach that tries to prevent bad outcomes – which is my view of how the current regulatory structure operates. We could change to one that, in my view, goes back to an earlier way of doing things. That would be an approach that emphasizes sanctions for fraudulent conduct but not necessarily to prevent bad outcomes. I frankly don't think that preventing bad outcomes is possible. When I took a class about securities investing many years ago, we called equities "risky assets" and the course was called "speculative markets." We didn't call securities investing "saving for retirement without risk."

In conclusion, the Order Handling Rules changed the way securities markets worked. In 1997, there may have been a reasonably accurate, short-term vision of what those changes would produce. But there was no particularly long-run clear vision by Rich or his staff of exactly as to where we would wind up today, or what this conference would be talking about in 2012.[15] The Order Handling Rules completely transformed what we did. The industry started working toward creating a long-term vision that didn't exist as a singular vision. The vision for the long term was that the resulting market structure would be created from everybody perusing their own incentives.

This afternoon, we will hear from a bunch of constituents at this conference – many of them are initiators. You have a confluence of catalyzers in place that I talked about already.

Change is coming. Change could easily be as dramatic as anything we have seen thus far, and that was put in place in the late 1990s. If we know anything about change, then we know exactly what form it takes and what is expected. So if you have questions, I would be happy to take them.

Harold Bradley [Former Chief Investment Officer, the Ewing Marion Kauffman Foundation] Frank, you are here today from NASDAQ. I would be remiss if I didn't ask, what do you see as changes or innovations after the Facebook problem?[16] Huge customer orders left unfilled, retail investors got plugged with orders from their brokers. Will this change the way retail distributors of IPOs – who thought they achieved a democratic nirvana in terms of access for their customers – will try and take control over the traditional underwriting process?

Hatheway I think the drivers for potential change in the IPO process transcend what happened on May 18, 2012, with the Facebook IPO – and I am avoiding any

[15] Refers to Dr. Richard Lindsey, formerly Director of Market Regulation and also Chief Economist at the US Securities and Exchange Commission. Lindsey, who presented the Opening Address at this conference as documented earlier in this book, oversaw the introduction of the Order Handling Rules at the Securities and Exchange Commission in 1997.

[16] Facebook's first day of trading on May 18, 2012, experienced serious technology setbacks that caused a delayed opening, resulting in thousands of orders being blocked for hours in NASDAQ's system. An estimated $500 million was lost by market-making firms and was a blow to NASDAQ which voluntarily repaid about $41.6 million to these firms. NASDAQ also agreed in April 23, 2015, to pay $26.5 million to settle a class-action lawsuit on behalf of retail investors in this same Facebook IPO.

specifics on that event. The process around the sale and placement of securities is old, so it satisfies that criterion on my list. It has participants who are in the current process and who aren't necessarily satisfied by it. It has people who are left out of the current process who definitely aren't satisfied by it. So, based on all the criteria that I have laid out today, the IPO process is ripe for change.

That said, the current IPO process has a very substantial set of established capital (both human and physical) that is difficult to change. The question becomes, where does the change come from? I don't think the IPO process is something where marginal change will be effective. If there's change, then it's revolutionary change. So where does it come from? Technologists can build books that allocate shares. For a technology solution to work, I think you need more of the fundamental, other types of revolutionary changes I was talking about in my concluding remarks.

I don't think technological change alone works. I don't think you see a significant change in how the IPO process works – unless you see a significant change in how the whole industry operates. In other words, it is more direct participation; it is not necessarily a replication of eBay, but it is closer to eBay-like. You can put in orders to buy shares – and nobody between you – and doing that is a big change.

Kenneth Pasternak [KABR Real Estate]: I entered the business in 1977 just when NASDAQ was coming into what is called adolescence. I saw an upstart marketplace that was built for entrepreneurs and growth companies and innovators. I dreamed of becoming an entrepreneur. I actually quit my good Wall Street job to try to be a CEO of a publicly traded company because I thought that was the neatest thing in the world. Today, I am talking to my 19-year-old son about opportunities in the world. You talk about the JOBS Act, but to me, as regards NASDAQ and the NYSE, I don't see much difference in what they are trying to do in market structure. NASDAQ thought about going back to this whole idea of what I call "capital formation." Do you see any kind of market structure that would facilitate the allocation of capital to early-stage companies similar to what occurred during the 1980s? Which I think was the heyday of NASDAQ when it supported early-stage companies, a service which kind of differentiated its marketplace from the NYSE.

Hatheway Yes, I think there is a gap in capital formation for small companies. And there is a theory of an academic colleague of Bob Schwartz and me. That says there is no capital formation gap, because entrepreneurs just create companies to be sold rather than to go public. I don't really buy the theory that entrepreneurs create a business to sell to the big companies as opposed to running their own shop like you wanted to do. To address that gap, NASDAQ has worked on an initiative called BX Venture.[17] BX Venture was started in 2008. Now NASDAQ is trying to understand and expand on what was created in the JOBS Act. We are interested in facilitating capital allocation. I am sure my competitors at the New York Stock Exchange are interested in it. But I am also sure that there are third parties who are not interested in it.

[17] Listing market for early-stage and small companies that do not qualify for listing on national securities exchanges.

Filling the gaps in raising capital gets into these interesting things that maybe are a more revolutionary outcome from the JOBS Act. You've got to change what we view as being the role of investing in speculative assets in the economy. You may have had conversations in DC where someone says that "people are putting their IRAs into stocks, so stocks have to be safe." I have had these conversations, and I just say stocks are risky and are not supposed to be safe. That is the whole point. That is what you are talking about.

Entrepreneurship is not supposed to be safe. Your business might have gone bust; maybe it went bust five times before it worked out. I don't know your history all that well. There is a role for that in society – and right now, the capital supporting that role is coming from the growing pools of money that are in the private equity space and venture capital. This type of investing is harder for an individual to participate in.

We lose something, both as a society and as individual employees, investors, and entrepreneurs, by not having the need for capital formation filled by the public markets. We have been working on it. We haven't been successful yet, and I hope we will be. I have a sneaking suspicion that it will be someone a lot younger than I am who comes up with the idea and makes it work. Thank you. [Applause]

Chapter 4
Regulators and Innovators as Initiators

Michael Pagano, Janet Angstadt, Tom Gira, Bill Harts, Keith Ross, and Robert Shapiro

Robert Schwartz Our next moderator, Michael Pagano, a fellow academician, is my very special colleague. Mike has clearly enhanced the practices and universe of academia. He is one of the few people who endured me as we worked together on five papers [laughter]. In my introduction earlier of Frank Hatheway, I cited a paper about empirical findings on NASDAQ calls – NASDAQ refers to them as "crossings" – and how these calls have made a positive contribution to markets. I produced this work with Mike, and also with one of my colleagues, Lin Peng, who is with us today. Let me also introduce Mike as a long-time friend. Please welcome him.

Michael Pagano Let's start with Keith Ross. Are you an initiator, an innovator, or are you both?

At time of writing, December 2014, Robert Shapiro had assumed a new role, Global Head of Trading and Execution Consulting at Bloomberg Tradebook.

M. Pagano (✉)
Villanova University, Villanova, PA, USA

J. Angstadt
Katten Muchin Rosenman LLP, Chicago, IL, USA

T. Gira
FINRA, Washington, DC, USA

B. Harts
Harts and Company, New York, NY, USA

K. Ross
PDQ Enterprises LLC, Glenview, IL, USA

R. Shapiro
Bloomberg Tradebook LLC, New York, NY, USA

R.A. Schwartz et al. (eds.), *Rapidly Changing Securities Markets*,
Zicklin School of Business Financial Markets Series,
DOI 10.1007/978-3-319-54588-2_4

Keith Ross After Frank Hatheway's eloquent presentation earlier today, my response is simple. We learned from Frank about innovators and initiators, and about how catalysts, marginalists, and technologists are all part of the same equation. In my view, regulators create the environment and they establish the boundaries for the innovators who initiate change. Over the last four decades, change has been significant and dramatic – and, I want to stress, the regulators initially created the environments. The innovators fall into place because of the opportunities created, and they do their best to innovate.

Robert Shapiro I agree with much of that. The innovators tend to be more flexible and work at a faster pace. You see a higher degree of initiation on their end. It seems that the innovators are more rapid in how they impact the regulatory market structure. Innovators often roll out or develop solutions that change and impact the marketplace. Regulators often make changes to market structure after an event – a Flash Crash, for example[1] – that demonstrates how change is necessary. In that context, the regulators can quite rapidly institute changes in market structure that can have a profound impact.

On the flip side of the coin, we have the regulatory time span. By that I mean the prolonged period of initiation – including an extended comment period – on proposed rules and regulations. It goes something like this: The SEC has panel presentations. Then the agency will ask market participants to comment on the proposed regulation. People will comment, the SEC will amalgamate these comments, and then put out another comment. In other words, there is a lot of back and forth, and change is an iterative process. In many instances, it can take years before this regulatory process finally culminates in rule and regulatory changes. Both of them, the innovators and the regulators, are impacting market structure for different reasons, and in response to different episodes in financial history.

Bill Harts When traders first enter the business, the limits to what they can do is drilled into their heads. These are the laws that govern our business; there is a wall here, a wall there. As long as you play in the middle of that space you will be fine. You can get pretty close to those limits or those walls and, as long as you don't cross them, you won't be fired – or go to jail. That is the way people in the industry are taught about the role of regulation.

The regulators themselves encourage that behavior by trying to put out very clear and robust sets of rules. But sometimes things happen that no one anticipated. "Wait a minute, maybe that wall shouldn't be there, maybe it should be a little closer," is the thinking. Suddenly, you find yourself on the wrong side of the wall and that leads to unintended consequences.

Tom Gira Being a regulator for 25 years now, I don't disagree with Kevin. However, let me set a framework. To make an analogy, it is basically like a canvas. The regulator sets the parameters, broadly, of what that canvas looks like. The regulator

---

[1] One of the most recent and most memorable: The May 6, 2010 Flash Crash when the Dow Jones Industrial Average dropped about 1000 points, or 9%, only to recover those losses within minutes. See, Findings Regarding The Market Events of May 6th, 2010, September 30, 2010. See, http://www.sec.gov/news/studies/2010/marketevents-report.pdf

might even offer the colors. But that doesn't mean the regulators will tell you exactly how you should use the paint. Regulators also more often than not tend to be a bit of a reactive factor. If you look at the Order Handling Rules[2] or Reg NMS,[3] or other rules that the Commission has instituted, it is usually because of some pent-up pressure, or event in the marketplace. With the Order Handling Rules, the Commission was reacting to how orders were mishandled in the marketplace, and then ECNs flourished because of the Order Handling Rules. Prior to Reg NMS, you had some markets that were fully electronic, and this just didn't mesh well with the manual trading on the NYSE.

Here's another analogy: The regulators are like a ship's captain, trying to point the ship in the right direction and attempting to guide it – aiming to create an environment that allows innovation and competition to flourish. But also involved are some overarching principles about fairness and integrity, about protecting investors, and promoting capital formation. But it requires tweaks. There is an iterative process between what happens in the markets and how this impacts regulations. As a general matter, it's a bit more reactive than proactive.

Janet Angstadt There has to be some continuity and stability of the regulatory framework so that market participants can plan and build businesses, all the while knowing that they will be operating within the existing rules. The SEC does play a big role in this, particularly when a proposed regulation is viewed as a differentiator among competitors. For example, an exchange doesn't typically want to impose obligations on its members, if such obligations may encourage its members to trade on another exchange. So, in some cases, it's necessary for the SEC to step in to introduce market-wide obligations.

Pagano Tom, as the only regulator on the panel, what are the motivations of a regulator relative to an innovator?

Gira We are engaged in a constant balancing act. Basically, this is our balancing act – promoting innovation while not fostering something that can be harmful to investors. When the Commission is considering hundreds and hundreds of comments on a proposal, it is never a one-size-fits-all situation. But, once again, there are some overarching principles about investor protection and capital formation; about facilitating orderly markets; about having rules that allow one to act quickly when there are bad actors in the marketplace.

A lot of events can occur that will change the course of market structure. For example, take the emergency rules with the Reg SHO rules in 2008.[4]

[2] The Order Handling Rules were introduced by the Securities and Exchange Commission in 1997. The rules included the Limit Order Display Rule and the Quote Rule and paved the way for today's "modern" high-speed electronic markets, starting with the early wave of upstart Electronic Communications Networks, or ECNs.

[3] Regulation National Market System (NMS) was enacted by the Securities and Exchange Commission in 2007 to foster competition among US exchanges and individual orders, and to promote fairness in price executions across all exchanges and platforms.

[4] Reg SHO, or Regulation SHO, enacted in January 2005, created "locate" and "close-out" standards mainly designed to prevent naked short-selling abuses. For the subsequent "emergency rules" in 2008, see, Securities Exchange Act of 1934 Release No. 58190/July 18, 2008 Amendment to Emergency Order Pursuant to Section 12(k)(2) of the Securities Exchange Act of 1934 Taking Temporary Action to Respond to Market Developments. http://edgar.sec.gov/rules/other/2008/34–58,190.pdf

Every event has its own unique circumstance. It is important to be thoughtful, to try to get as much input and dialog as possible. But after you take the first step, it is very hard to put the toothpaste back in the tube.

Pagano Rob, from the innovation side, what are your thoughts on that? In general, what is your perspective on how to navigate?

Shapiro We like to build cool things that people will use – that's what motivates us – as well as making money on some level. But, I don't know what motivates the regulators. Their job seems incredibly difficult given how many masters they have to serve. Their job is a constant balancing act. When you talk about innovation, or about innovators as initiators, the motivations are quite simple. You want to bring products to market that are safe, that are commercial, and that you believe in. And you want to have the luxury of doing that quickly with enough capital, with the right people, and with a plan of execution.

Our firm has a very rigorous vetting process around ideas. I would imagine that it is far less difficult to get an idea to market at Tradebook than it is to advance one of these major regulatory edicts at the SEC. We have already alluded to the fact that it could take months, if not years, at the regulatory level.

Pagano In other words, right now it is much nimbler on that side of the fence when it comes to the regulatory issues. I knew we wouldn't get too far into this panel until the famous words, "unintended consequences," had to come up. Bill, what are some of the biggest unintended consequences of the regulatory changes that we have covered today? Let's start with the Order Handling Rules, and then continue with decimalization,[5] Reg ATS,[6] Reg NMS,[7] MiFID, and MiFID II.[8]

Harts The one unintended consequence that regulators didn't quite foresee is the incredible amount of fragmentation fostered by some of the rules. At last count, there are 40 venues available for trading US equities, including dark pools and exchanges, ATSs, and ECNs.[9] We shouldn't be micromanaging the regulatory process. You will never be able to predict all the things that could possibly happen. A lighter touch is better, while still trying to guarantee the safety of investors.

[5] US markets were legally required and then switched from trading in fractional increments to decimal pricing in 2001.

[6] Reg ATS, or Regulation ATS, enacted by the SEC in 1998, regulates the various Alternative Trading Systems in the US markets, including Electronic Communications Networks, or ECNs.

[7] Reg NMS, or Regulation NMS, enacted in 2007 by the Securities and Exchange Commission, aims to improve the quality of US market structure through significant enhancements in price executions and quoting processes, increment size, and market data. Specifically, there are four distinct rules in Reg NMS: order protection for investors so they can get the best price anywhere with the elimination of trade-throughs; improved access to quotations in the National Markets System via enhanced linkages and lower access fees; sub-penny trading on securities; and finally, market data reform that allocates formula-based revenues to market centers that offer improved access to market data.

[8] Markets in Financial Instruments Directive I, or MiFID I, introduced in October 2010, was followed by the second MiFID proposals, or MiFID II, in September 2012, aiming for the reform and harmonization of European area markets. MiFID II shifts the European regulatory regime from a principles-based to a more US-style, rules-based regulatory model.

[9] At the time of writing, there were some 45 ATSs and 13 public securities exchanges.

In practical terms, the list of unintended consequences is long. I am sure that everyone here has stories.

Let me mention one other thing. People were talking about how the recent action in Kraft Foods[10] led to a front page story in *The Wall Street Journal*, and to television coverage. Most people in this room know that errors have happened since probably the beginning of organized trading. When I listen to talk about the markets being dysfunctional, it occurs to me that a better way to put it would be that they are hyperfunctional. Things happen so quickly, and liquidity moves so fast. We have an unprecedented amount of transparency, so much so that almost anyone who is looking at the markets today can form an opinion on what's happening when you have things like the Kraft or the Knight[11] situations.

Angstadt Interestingly, one of the reasons there are so many market venues for equities is because the SEC wanted to encourage innovation and competition. It has led us to this place where we have so many different equity exchanges and dark pools. The number of equities venues can be viewed as the result of the SEC's policy of not standing in the way of innovation and technology.

Gira Maybe sometimes we are too hard on ourselves in terms of the market. There is certainly fragmentation. But the markets are much more linked today than they ever were before. Look at how all of the exchanges, dark pools, ATSs, and other trading venues are electronically linked today through broker dealer routing systems. Long gone are the days when your Intermarket Trading System commitments[12] would go to an exchange and they would sit there for 2 min and be ignored. It is important to recognize the benefits of the current market. While it is fragmented from a volume standpoint, it is actually fairly well linked from a connectivity standpoint.

---

[10] Kraft Hit by Trading Glitch, Alexandra Scaggs and Matt Jarzemsky, *Wall Street Journal*, October 3, 2012. According to the opening paragraph: "Investors were hit with another stock-trading glitch Wednesday, this one in a house name – Kraft Foods – which saw dozens of trades canceled when a broker errors caused shares to soar shortly after the opening bell." http://www.wsj.com/articles/SB10000872396390443768804578034354197596528

[11] August 1 stock trading fiasco costs Knight $604M, *USA Today*, October 17, 2012. According to the opening paragraph in this AP story: "The Knight Capital Group trading firm said it lost $764.3 million in the third quarter because of a software glitch that flooded the stock market with trades one day in August, causing dozens of stocks to fluctuate wildly." http://www.usatoday.com/story/money/markets/2012/10/17/knight-capital-earnings/1638817/

[12] "Electronic communications network linking the trading floors of seven registered exchanges to permit trading among them in stocks listed on either the NYSE or AMEX and one or more regional exchanges. Through ITS, any broker or market maker on the floor of any participating exchange can reach other participants for an execution whenever the nationwide quote shows a better price available. A floor broker on the exchange can enter an ITS order to assure excecution of all of an offering or bid, instead of splitting it with competing brokers."

Source: NASDAQ. See, http://www.nasdaq.com/investing/glossary/i/intermarket-trading-system#ixzz3S78pIeH9

General reference on "commitments" in this Federal Register notice, 15 August, 2001: Intermarket Trading System; Notice of Filing of the Seventeenth Amendment to the ITS Plan Relating to Regional Computer Interface, 30-Second Commitment Expiration, and the Principal Place of Business of the Boston Stock Exchange, Inc. https://www.federalregister.gov/articles/2001/08/15/01-20500/intermarket-trading-system-notice-of-filing-of-the-seventeenth-amendment-to-the-its-plan-relating-to

The fragmentation that needs our focus is the regulatory fragmentation. When you have order flow dispersed over so many different marketplaces, it is very hard to get a holistic view of the markets. The Commission is taking a very proactive step by proposing the Consolidated Audit Trail, commonly known as the CAT.[13] As exchanges have become for-profit, they have looked to FINRA[14] to outsource some of their regulatory obligations. As a result, FINRA is increasingly becoming an industry utility for surveillance, and it has been able to put the pieces together for a more holistic view of the market. We have seen instances where firms will consciously spread their activity across multiple markets to avoid detection.

Pagano We have a question from a very shy fellow!

Harold Bradley [Former Chief Investment Officer, The Ewing Marion Kauffman Foundation] Yesterday, there was an interesting story in *The New York Times* about the SEC employing Tradeworx to write something called an "algorithm hunter."[15] Explain to me how that will help the regulator. What will the SEC accomplish with a live trading venue? Help me to understand how FINRA, or the SEC, will benefit from that kind of algorithmic development.

Gira I don't work at the SEC anymore, but I will try to give you my perspective. The Commission traditionally has not used surveillance tools to deter bad behavior. They rely on referrals from the SROs,[16] tips, complaints, whistleblowers, referrals from other areas with the Commission, and their analysis of market events. When matters are on the SEC's radar screen, they have very effective investigative tools and techniques. But traditionally there have not been many SEC systems to detect potentially problematic trading. Thus, I see the SEC's use of Tradeworks as a good first step to becoming more knowledgeable about the markets. Greg Berman[17] at the SEC, who is leading this effort, is extremely intelligent. I am sure he will generate a lot of good empirical work that will help the SEC. Unfortunately, the SEC's analysis will be somewhat constrained because it is my understanding that Tradeworks will be relying on publicly available data, not on data where the SEC would know the parties to trades. Nevertheless, I think it will allow the Commission to be a lot more informed than they are today.

---

[13] See SEC Press Release, July 11, 2012: Approves New Rule Requiring Consolidated Audit Trail to Monitor and Analyze Trading Activity. http://www.sec.gov/News/PressRelease/Detail/PressRelease/1365171483188

For a discussion on kill switches at 2012 Securities and Exchange Commission Round Table: http://www.marketwatch.com/story/panel-at-sec-backs-high-speed-trading-kill-switch-2012-10-02

[14] The Financial Industry Regulatory Authority, or FINRA, is the US securities industry's largest independent regulator. http://www.finra.org/AboutFINRA/WhatWeDo/

[15] To Regulate Rapid Traders, SEC. Turns to One of Them, Nathaniel Popper and Ben Protess, *New York Times*, October 2, 2012. http://www.nytimes.com/2012/10/08/business/sec-regulators-turn-to-high-speed-trading-firm.html?pagew

[16] Self-regulatory organizations.

[17] At the time of writing, Greg Berman is Associate Director, Office of Analytics and Research at the SEC and was at the agency's Trading and Markets Division at the time of this conference.

On the FINRA side, we now regulate 80% of the market between the NASDAQ family markets, and the New York family markets, and the over-the-counter market, and we have expanded our OATS rule.[18] For 80% of the market, we can now see orders from cradle to grave. As part of New York Stock Exchange coming on board with FINRA back in 2010, we revamped all of the surveillance patterns we had in place and relaunched them in 2012 with the ability to monitor multiple markets simultaneously.

We used to have a pattern that looked for front running on Arca – and just on Arca. We had another front-running pattern just for NASDAQ, and yet another one just for the NYSE. Now we have one pattern that brings data together from all these exchanges, and it looks across all markets. It is not perfect – we still don't have OATS rules that are applied universally to all market participants. But that is coming with the SEC's CAT plan approved in July.[19]

Harts Is CAT an extension of OATS, or is OATS going to be discontinued?

Gira As the CAT rules have just been approved, and because the SROs now have to approve the CAT, those issues are still to be determined.

Shapiro Can you tell us what CAT is?

Gira CAT stands for the Consolidated Audit Trail.[20] Basically, CAT will track an order from cradle to grave. And it will allow you to know when it was canceled, was executed, or if it was executed in parts. One of the more controversial things about it is that regulators also will know the customer ID associated with the order. If a customer has multiple accounts at multiple firms, even that will all map into one account number. CAT will also include options orders, which are not captured today until they are entered into exchange systems. This is all in the formative stages. When completed, you will have an even playing field in terms of orders, quotes, and trades being collected across all of the marketplaces.

The exchanges and FINRA are working together to develop such a plan. We at FINRA think that OATS could be the foundation on which CAT can be built. But by no means is OATS the equivalent to CAT. And there could be other systems out there as well. There is a perception that OATS was built in the 1990s, and that it hasn't kept up with technology. I am not sure that is a fair perception and, personally, I think that it is better to leverage something that we already have.

[18] OATS, or the Order Audit Trail System, was created by the NASD to accurately record time sensitive information pertaining to the events in the order execution process.

[19] See, SEC Approves New Rule Requiring Consolidated Audit Trail to Monitor and Analyze Trading Activity. (footnote 13). http://www.sec.gov/News/PressRelease/Detail/PressRelease/1365171483188

[20] See, SEC proposes Consolidated Audit Trail System to Better Track Market Trades, SEC Press Release, May 26, 2010. http://www.sec.gov/news/press/2010/2010–86.htm

Neal Wolkoff [Wolkoff Consulting Services, LLC.] What do you think about the role of exchanges as SRO's with real-time market management? Tom was just talking about the ability to recreate a market, as I understand it, after the fact. But we've seen from the Flash Crash that one of the issues involved the NYSE having liquidity replenishment points, or LRPs, that other exchanges didn't have.[21] We are now talking about exchanges having kill switches.[22] But there really isn't any formal mechanism for the markets to make these decisions in a collective manner. They are independent, for-profit operations. The structure is inconsistent because something could happen on one market, on a third market, on a ninth market, on a seventh market.

I would hate to think that the SEC buying the Tradeworx application is signifying that the SEC plans to become the real-time market monitor. I am curious about whether the exchanges in the marketplace, or the SROs, are still able to be the real-time monitor of trading now that it is automated and dispersed across multiple venues.

Gira Clearly, exchanges now need to look at some issues differently given the fragmentation in the market. The implementation of market-wide trading pauses that were developed after May 6 and the development of the limit up-limit down proposals that are scheduled to go into effect in February 2013 are both very good examples that illustrate how the exchanges actually are much more cooperative today in trying to prevent and minimize extreme market volatility.[23] Before the SEC's Roundtable last week,[24] a couple of the exchanges and FINRA also submitted comment letters about whether kill switches should be in place at the exchanges. Right now, if one exchange kills a firm, you must have immediate communication with the others.

It could get ugly if the firm who gets killed really didn't want to be killed. But there is actually a mention in a letter to another mechanism that could possibly get us to a better, multilayered risk management approach. Earlier today, Frank Hatheway of NASDAQ mentioned how the clearing side has been kind of stale, and I think that is probably true. But maybe one way to have a better, more holistic risk management tool during extreme volatility is to have a kill switch at the clearing house level. A lot of issues are associated with that too.

[21] See, NYSE Pressure Valve Highlighted in Plunge, Steven D. Jones, *Wall Street Journal*, May 07, 2010, http://www.wsj.com/articles/SB10001424052748704370704575229092263818572

[22] See explanatory related story related, NYSE proposes "kill switch" to help catch trading errors, John McCrank, December 23, 2013, *Reuters*. "IntercontinentalExchange Group's NYSE Euronext unit has filed a plan with regulators to offer firms that trade on the New York Stock Exchange a 'kill switch' that could cut off trading if preset levels were breached," according to this story. http://finance.yahoo.com/news/nyse-proposes-kill-switch-help-193900601.html

[23] The proposal moved forward and was implemented. See, SEC Press Release, April 5, 2011: SEC Announces Filing of Limit Up-Limit Down Proposal to Address Extraordinary Market Volatility. http://www.sec.gov/news/press/2011/2011–84.htm

[24] See, SEC ROUNDTABLE: Kill switches and Best Practices Are Coming. John D'Antona Jr., *Traders Magazine*, October 2, 2012. "The implementation of so-called 'kill switches' and a uniform best practices guide to electronic trading stand as the two high points of Tuesday's Securities and Exchange Commission roundtable meeting," according to the story.

Ross I was at a conference in Hong Kong this past summer where many exchanges were represented. The big question at the conference was, who hits the switch? And at what level? The exchanges don't know customers' assets, but the broker dealers on the front lines do.[25] So, if an exchange sees some kind of activity, might they hit the switch incorrectly? The broker dealer may not have all of a client's business, but they know the client's assets that reside with them. This issue has a lot of complications, including the legal implications that sit on top of the regulatory issues. For example, what are the agreements with the exchange, the broker dealers, and their customers, and their clients?

Angstadt There already is a kill switch of sorts embedded in the SEC's market access rules. A broker dealer must have an aggregate credit threshold limit for their clients. A client that attempts to exceed the limit should be blocked. There has hopefully been some discussion between broker dealers and their clients on what those thresholds should be. I view that, at least on the client level, as a way to stop the damage if there is a problem.

Harts If there was a circuit breaker, wouldn't the NYSE say that trading imbalances on the NYSE are our proprietary information? That's what makes our market. We know that there is an imbalance, and now a regulator will force us to share that information with all of our competitors? I don't see it happening.

Pagano Are we losing the basic purpose of what you should be doing with an exchange? Or with the market in general?

Ross It was noted that price formation is the most important thing the marketplace contributes. The question is, price formation for whom, and in what time frame?

Shapiro This is what is being alluded to. The exchanges are for-profit. It begs the question that everyone asks, shouldn't the markets be in the business of price formation for the retail investor? If that was in the exclusive domain of an exchange, you could suggest that they wouldn't be doing a lot of business in aggregate.

There are new models coming out that are starting to address price formation for certain segments of the marketplace on an exclusive basis.[26] That brings us to another point. Very often, innovators who are entrepreneurs start solving the problems of the market dynamically. If there is, in fact, a real need for price formation for the exclusive benefit of plain-vanilla institutional investors (who are usually a proxy for retail), those solutions are coming to the market as we speak. But it is hard to answer the

---

[25] As Ross elaborated in a follow-up interview, exchanges will not know the funding of an account of an investor sending orders. The exchange will not know if the investor has billions or thousands of dollars, or just a nominal amount in the account.

[26] Shapiro, in a follow-up interview, noted how there are new models starting to address price formation for certain segments of the marketplace. In this instance, that means "exclusively" for ETFs, according to Shapiro. One example close to home for Shapiro is Bloomberg Tradebook's own ETF RFQ platform, which was officially launched in 2014. See, Press Release (October 15, 2014), Bloomberg Tradebook First to Aggregate Buy-side Liquidity in ETF. http://www.bloomberg.com/now/press-releases/bloomberg-tradebook-first-aggregate-buy-side-liquidity-etfs/

question in the spirit it was asked. It is, at least to my ears, implied that the market should have some form of ethical responsibility for price formation in a classic context.

Everything is different now. I am not sure how you solve the romantic vision of that question against the needs of a high-frequency trading firm that wants to colocate within 2 inches of your server, and process trades at supersonic speed.[27]

Unknown How do we discover in this new world what, for example, it is worth to know IBM's price? What is the right price for IBM at a certain volume?

Ross The reason people trade is because they either have a different concept of the valuation of the security, or they have a different time frame.[28] The high-frequency crowd is not as concerned about the fundamental value of IBM as is Warren Buffet. They are trying to balance the supply and demand in the market place – and they can earn a fee for providing liquidity. I think of it as a service they provide. If they are successful, they get paid for it. If they are not successful, they don't.

There was a comment earlier about the call auction. PDQ ATS offers an auction for every order that is interested. Our clients will also request that their orders be paused for a relatively brief period of time, during which we can aggregate the market based on their needs, their size, and the liquidity they are looking for.[29]

Unknown [Audience] How would you educate the customer, the retail guy? How will a retail customer know if he has received the right price for his shares?

Pagano You are referring to a public good. That is to say, when you trade, not only do you have the benefit of two parties buying and selling the security, but you have information about the price that many nonparticipants can benefit from. In economic terms, we call this a positive externality. I don't have to be part of that trade as long as information about it is publically revealed. When I see the price, I know something about the value of IBM.

The idea of a public good is your point. You may know it is good for everybody, but not everybody bears the cost of making the trade. The question boils down to, who should be paying to provide that public good service? And should the regulator step in and do something?

---

[27] Colocate refers here to the much debated practice of "colocation" by high-frequency trading, or HFT firms, of their computerized boxes next to an exchange server, placed there for the advantage of split second price trading data feeds. Most investors, by contrast, get their price data feeds slightly later through consolidated prices, via the market. The New York Stock Exchange, indeed, has made substantial revenue from colocation services.

[28] In a follow-up interview, Ross elaborated that the classic buy-and-hold investor does not buy or sell in a rapid-fire fashion similar to a HFT firm. By the same token, the legendary Warren Buffett is typically not concerned about the performance of his new investment over, say, the next 5 min, rather he is likely weighing up his investment and its fundamental value on a much longer time horizon measured in years, buying at 20, for example, patiently waiting for it to rise to 30 and above, or to gain substantially in value.

[29] In a follow-up interview Ross noted that the "value proposition" of PDQ ATS is that the decision of how the trade takes place should be "client driven." Among its services, PDQ introduced a one-second auction so that if clients are willing to wait for the platform to aggregate liquidity, then that elapsed time can be used to source liquidity from other venues, and from other asset players.

Gira Reg NMS has the trade-through rule. The rule means you can't trade through somebody else's quote. You also have a best execution obligation. The other question should be about obtaining price improvement. Our current environment is one where best execution changes over time depending on the market structure. There are some principals involved – if you are handling a customer order you are obligated to get the best price possible.

Angstadt In addition, there is unprecedented transparency for retail investors. They can see real-time prices today. In some cases, they can see some depth of book. Real-time quote and last sale transparency is an important tool for retail investors to protect themselves.

Harts I am glad Tom brought up the term "best execution." I have heard about this term for the past 20 years. Yet, as far as I know – Tom, maybe you can correct me – no one single enforcement action has ever been brought by the commission against a firm for failure to achieve best execution. Is everybody getting it right?

Gira We actually do bring best execution cases at FINRA. We bring actions for violations on two horizons – a price horizon and a time horizon. The best execution rules say that you have to take reasonable efforts to get the best price possible for the customer under the circumstances. If somebody has traded through a market and hasn't complied with the rule – and the customer gets an inferior execution – we do bring those cases. The other type of best execution case we bring are market order timeliness cases. Here if an order has taken too long to be executed, and the market moves against the order while it is pending, we will say it is a best execution violation.

Bernard Donefer [Baruch College] I want to talk again about the kill switch. If we look at Knight's problem on August 1, the NYSE recognized the problem within the first 2 min of the unusual activity. It notified Knight about the very high volumes. You might say, well, is there somebody who should have stopped trading? They have DMMs[30] on the floor of the exchange whose job is to do just that. So there were at least 10 or more DMMs who had a positive obligation to look at a market open if it appeared anomalous. There was not a single DMM on the floor who acted during the entire period.

When you talk about putting in a kill switch – and getting somebody to actually pull the plug on trading – it is worth remembering that you had all of these people at the primary market watching it happen. And no one was doing anything about it. Do we even need DMMs? What is their job? What is their purpose?

Shapiro What does that tell you?

Donefer That kill switches won't necessarily be the answer. Somebody has to make a decision, and everyone is dancing around it. Nobody wants to make a decision.

Shapiro Let's put this another way. Perhaps the complexity of the marketplace has outstripped the ability of some people who have a fiduciary responsibility to prevent these events from impacting price formation. Why? Because you really don't know

[30] Designated Market Makers, or DMMs, are NYSE "market makers" obliged to maintain fair and orderly markets in a specific group of listed stocks.

a so-called six-sigma event is occurring until it is in the rearview mirror. When a cataclysmic event happens, there's no way to have predicted that the event would happen. We can only try to understand it after the fact.

When we talk about the unintended consequences of Reg NMS, it brings the panel back to the topic we are here to talk about. The number one unintended consequence is the complexity of our markets. You can talk about fragmentation. You can talk about lower share volume. This is all just complexity in aggregate. Things have become incredibly complex. I just picked this up off the display table. There is an article in the latest *Journal of Trading* on Dynamic Density Estimation of Market Microstructure Variables via Auxiliary Particle Filtering.[31]

Harts That is a great article. [laughter]

Shapiro It is a great article, right? It has gotten that extreme, and a lot of us, yours truly included, struggle trying to figure out how to make sense of this market, and how to do our jobs. Almost everybody is a fiduciary on some level. You have to understand that some things are really beyond one's core experience, or that they are moving too fast for you to keep up. The regulators are probably being more honest than most. They are also spending time and money, and are not ashamed about calling in experts from private industry to help them get on top of the stuff. In another way, this leads me to believe that entrepreneurs and the private sector tend to help the regulators, almost hand in hand, to manage the fluctuation of market structure in the wake of big events like Reg NMS.

Harts To clarify, they were obviously not Knight DMMs that were watching the stock?

Shapiro Right.

Harts There was another company. The NYSE DDM reportedly called Knight, and Knight said no, that as far as they knew, everything was fine. We have free markets. People are able to do what they want. They can trade how they want to trade, even if it is due to a mistake and could even put a company out of business. That is the way it works, right? That is what happened here.

Donefer Unfortunately, yes, but at what point does a DMM actually act?

Harts Maybe a DMM should be automated too.

Gira There has to be multiple safety nets to prevent the market from extreme volatility. But the root cause is the creation of trading algorithms that can wreak havoc on the market. We see a lot of varied practices in how firms introduce their algos, and in how they test them. Some firms give their developers wide latitude to tinker with their algorithms. And, as a result, the firms sometimes don't really know what they are releasing on the markets. Other firms have it locked down, and don't launch anything until it is firmly tested. Some firms will turn their algos off if they are making too much money, or too little money. Overall, there needs to be

[31] Dynamic Density Estimation of Market Microstructure Variables via Auxiliary Particle Filtering. Daniel Nehren, David Fellah, Jesus Ruiz-Mata, Yichen Qin. *Journal of Trading*. Vol 7, No 4 (2012).

much more rigorous, robust testing before automated trading algorithms are used or modified. And they need to be followed up on, not just prior to launch but after the launch as well.

Then it is a matter of how to contain trading once a trading algorithm goes haywire, or there is a human error in entering an order. The SEC's direct market access rule focuses on the role of the broker dealer. I think that we are learning that some other layers are needed as well – like the exchanges.

Donefer Most of the algos are tested very well. But an algo that works well 249 days out of the year can go crazy on that 250th day, which is what happened on the May 10th Flash Crash.[32]

Gira That is true probably 99.9% of the time. But we also have to better integrate the developer and the trader. Sometimes, frankly, the compliance staffs at some of the high-frequency trading firms are not keeping up. They don't know what the traders are doing. They need to know. We have also seen instances where you tell a firm to give us all your market making algos, and they can't do that. They can't necessarily identify what the algos are for. This is calling out for best practices in terms of testing and controls.

Pagano Bob has been waiting patiently.

Schwartz I am used to waiting patiently because I like call auctions [laughter and applause]! I would like to circle back to a thought: What is the function of an exchange? Back in the traditional, bygone days, an exchange was a big part of the marketplace. If you are talking about regulation, what Bernard Donefer is talking about, the fragility of markets is, quite obviously, terribly important. If you take more of an aerial view and look, not just at the trees, but at the forest, what then does an exchange look like? What is its product? What does it produce? It reminds me of something I have mentioned at previous conferences.

There was a discussion at the NYSE many years ago when Mil Batton, predecessor of John Phelan, was Chairman of the exchange, a post Mil held until 1984. The discussion was about what does the exchange produce? What is its service? I sat there in silence and listened. Mil Batton was also a listener, he wasn't just a talker. When he did speak up, he said, quite simply, "we produce the price!" Now, what am I circling back to? I am circling back to price discovery. It gets underplayed in public discussion because it is so extremely difficult to assess the quality of price discovery. What is our benchmark? Only God knows the equilibrium price.

But there are manifestations of poorly discovered prices. The manifestation that I focus on is intraday volatility which, on an ongoing basis, appears to be strikingly high. So, am I asking a question, or am I making a statement? A little of both, no doubt. If you would like to pick up on that, I would be interested.

Ross I would not only add price, Bob, but also liquidity. So the price is not terribly relevant if it is for a hundred dollars' worth of the security.

---

[32] See footnote 1.

Schwartz Then it's not well discovered, for sure.

Ross Correct, but it if is for a million dollars' worth of the security, and if the bid-ask spread is a fraction of a percent, then the exchanges is doing its job. Certainly the harnessing of technology, to make trading more efficient, is a huge accomplishment due to the change in regulation over the last 15 years.

The firm I was formerly with was very active in high-speed trading before Reg NMS was enacted. We had discussions with the regulators at the highest levels. We were explaining to them that the market landscape was going to change very dramatically if they did enact Reg NMS. All the markets had to be linked, with quotes being protected and so forth. We said this would change the lives of the dealers and the specialists. The comment from the regulators was, "we know this" – and the NYSE specialists will have to deal with it. Now we are finding that there are all other kinds of issues and unintended consequences. Now we have to try and deal with them.

Schwartz Tom, to what extent does this subject come up at FINRA? Do you pay attention to the quality of price discovery?

Gira The issue of price discovery and the attributes of an exchange do come up at FINRA, in the context of caring about investor protection and market integrity. FINRA is running the over-the-counter market from a statutory perspective. We are obligated to have a quoting mechanism which is the Alternative Display Facility,[33] but it is dormant. We also collect trade reports and conduct surveillance of the OTC markets, but our involvement with price discovery and other exchange-related issues is mostly related to our regulation of exchange markets.

We try to regulate the exchanges as best we can. We are not in their business, but we will inform them of market developments and observations when we see things. However, we are not trying to dictate to them what their market structures should be.

Schwartz Yes, I would certainly expect that. Will you make the CAT data available to academicians? More specifically, will you get it to Mike Pagano so I can do another paper with him?

Gira Unfortunately, we are probably years away from answering that question. It will take a while to build the system.

Schwartz And we are always years away from publishing the paper. [laughter]

[33] "The Alternative Display Facility (ADF) is an SRO display only facility that is operated by FINRA. The ADF provides members with a facility for the display of quotations, the reporting of trades, and the comparison of trades. ADF best bid and offer and trade reports are included in the consolidated data stream for NASDAQ and CQS listed securities. As an SRO display only facility, ADF does not provide automated order routing functionality, execution facilities, or linkages between ADF trading centers. ADF trading centers are required by FINRA rule to provide direct electronic access to all other ADF trading centers and provide such access to all FINRA members that request it. All FINRA members in good standing are eligible to participate in ADF, pending execution of appropriate contracts and meeting specific requirements as set forth by FINRA." Source: FINRA. See, http://www.finra.org/Industry/Compliance/MarketTransparency/ADF/index.htm

Gira Switching gears, someone asked the question about trading pauses when the market hits a certain level and trading stops. That is a pretty blunt instrument. It is complex in the terms of how it operates, with the limit up-limit down mechanism that will be implemented. Basically, there will be moving price bands calculated for each stock throughout the day. The bands will be based on movements in the stock's average price during discrete time periods. If the price of a stock hits a level a certain percentage away from where it was a few moments earlier and bounces off it, the market will remain open. If the price hits that point and doesn't bounce off it, then the stock will go into a trading pause.[34]

Pagano One last question?

Tim Lang [Global Liquidity Partners] I want to agree with Keith. Besides price, more importantly today in fractional markets, the question is, where is the liquidity? Some electronic services firms just do algorithms for institutional, buy-side and sell-side clients. Sixty percent of all market orders from these algorithms fill in the non-lit markets.[35] The big issue I see today from our clients is defining best execution on a 100,000-share order. Best execution rules need updating for the institutional order executed in 50 different places. It is easy on retail orders, but what about an order that is running through a VWAP[36] all day? When my execution is compared to, say Barclays or Goldman Sachs, they could see a 2, 3, 5 cent difference based on where the liquidity was. My clients don't know how to define best execution. And I don't want to beat up on the regulator. My name is John Smith! [laughter]

Harts Here's something else: We haven't talked a lot about market data. Let's be clear, the fees generated from market data might be the grease that is lubricating all of these market structure changes. Just a few weeks ago, the NYSE was fined a significant amount of money for transmitting their prices to the consolidated tape at a slower pace than required, maybe it was 500 microseconds slower. They were transmitting to their proprietary data feed customers. How fast, I ask, is too fast? Let's keep in mind that it is not just about how fast the orders get there, it is also about how fast the attending price discovery is disseminated.

Pagano We had a very good, wide-ranging discussion here, especially with regulators and innovators on this panel today. Thank you all. [applause]

---

[34] As of writing, in terms of percentage movements in stock prices, a trading halt was triggered if a price rose or fell more than 5% over a 5-min period in the most heavily traded shares. The price band was widened to 10% to generate a halt in the second stage of the roll-out.

[35] The order books are publicly available to subscribers.

[36] Volume weighted average price.

Chapter 5
A Walk Through Time

Harold Bradley

Robert Schwartz I have a complete collection of vintage Harold Bradley stories I am saving for the cocktail hour later. Harold and I have had so much fun and good times together at any number of conferences both here in the USA and in Europe. Our thoughts about market structure are, as I would "call" it, quite compatible. Yes, pun intended! Many of you are no doubt familiar with my support for call auctions! [laughter]. So, that aside, it is my great pleasure to introduce Harold Bradley, one of our foremost thinkers on market structure. Let me warn you: Harold has a penchant for speaking his mind – and I am sure he won't disappoint us today.

Harold Bradley About five years ago, Bob was recognized by Baruch College for his major academic contributions. Bob has now invited me to talk at this great conference today. How time flies. It has made me realize how long our friendship has endured. We met each other about the same time I was forming relationships with many of the same industry leaders and contributors who are here today, Richard Lindsey and Janet Angstadt included.

Time is important in the context of market structure. If you want a good sense of the rapid pace of industry change, read *Market 2000*,[1] a really thick book published in 1994 that reflected the comments gathered by the Securities and Exchange Commission from the industry on issues relating to the regulation of market structure. I keep it proudly today in a special place on my bookshelf. The report laid out a regulatory framework that played out over more than 18 years. Janet co-authored it as a young attorney with Howard Kramer, when they were both at the SEC, she reminds me. Janet, you were just 15 at the time! [laughter]

[1] *Market 2000*: An Examination of Current Equity Market Developments. Division of Market Regulation, US Securities and Exchange Commission, January 1994.

H. Bradley (✉)
The Ewing Marion Kauffman Foundation, Kansas City, MO, USA

R.A. Schwartz et al. (eds.), *Rapidly Changing Securities Markets*, Zicklin School of Business Financial Markets Series,
DOI 10.1007/978-3-319-54588-2_5

Here is what is really interesting about that now – and this is front running my presentation! I believe there were only 50 Comment Letters filed by industry practitioners, mostly lawyers – and only a total of four filed by buy-side firms on questions raised in the *Market 2000* study. The subsequent published report shocked many of the same industry participants who were systematically mute in their interactions with the Commission. Actually, I filed a 45-page summary paper filled with data on electronic trading – following up on the request for data in the release – and the SEC didn't receive data from anybody else. I was pretty amazed. So I learned that early on – and for the next 20 years I would come loaded with data to show folks how things work.

Of course, Bob Schwartz invited me to this luncheon talk today with the same low-key, rope-a-dope routine he performed for Rich Lindsey earlier. "Harold, just show up; you don't have to prepare. Just talk about the good old days," Bob quipped. Needless to say, all stories are better with a bit of data and history sprinkled on top.

I have titled my talk, "A Walk Through Time…From Evil SOES Bandits and to Evil High-Frequency Traders and the Intermediaries' Constant Claims on the Public Goods." My entire career is marked by rapid, disruptive changes to the world equity markets or, as Mark Twain put it, history doesn't repeat itself, it rhymes. I live and have spent my entire career in Kansas City. I worked for 20 years at American Century Mutual Funds where I was head of trading. American Century was probably the first firm on the buy-side to completely automate our trading processes. One of my mentees, I guy I love dearly, later went on to become CEO of Archipelago,[2] a guy named Mike Cormack. Mike went to work in the customer service department of Twentieth Century[3] when he graduated from John Hopkins University. I originally met him when he won a company-wide contest to be a trader for a day at Twentieth Century – and he soon won my admiration and respect.

Back in the early 90s, as a buy-side firm, it was in the DNA of James Stowers, Twenthieth Century's founder and his son, that we should not be giving orders to Wall Street because the Street didn't treat them right. Which goes back to Frank Hatheway's talk today about who are the instigators. It comes to the fore when participants realize they aren't getting a good deal in the bargain they are paying for.

This was my trading badge in the early days of my career [holds badge aloft]. In 1984, I bought a membership at the Kansas City Board of Trade (KCBT) to trade stock index futures. I did so after spending two years explaining Value Line index futures to the world. By the way, does anybody know where the first cash settled stock index futures contract traded? No? See, it is all lost to history.

Audience Member Kansas City.

[2] Chicago-based Archipelago Exchange was acquired by the New York Stock Exchange in January 2006. Cormack made the transition to the NYSE but stepped down later in the same year as an executive vice president at the NYSE Group, remaining on as a "senior consultant."

[3] American Century changed its name from Twentieth Century in the 1990s.

Bradley Yes, Kansas City. And guess what happened back then and why Rich Lindsey, who spoke today at the conference, pursued his work at the Securities and Exchange Commission. As soon as a small exchange innovated, it took us as long as six years to get through the regulatory process at the SEC and the Commodity Futures Trading Commission. Once we had the contract approved, what happened next? All the barriers to competitors fell down. The Chicago Mercantile Exchange introduced the S&P 500 within weeks.

Back then, innovation in regulated financial markets proved to be practically impossible. Established exchanges fought any attempts to change the rules of the game – and quickly coopted any innovation that survived the regulatory bludgeon. The excessive time, money and persistence, required by folks trying to make the markets better, never seemed to reward the innovator.

My experience with both the Kansas City Board of Trade and the Midwest Stock Exchange as relentless innovators who failed to win, inspired many of my longest held views about competition in the markets. I viewed decimalization[4] and the Order Handling Rules[5] as important skirmishes in the pursuit of markets that benefit the investors of capital – and not the intermediaries of other people's money. So that is one of my biases.

I was a local in the crowd for five years at the KCBT and, as I noted already, I spread traded Value Line and S&P 500 futures.[6] But let's talk about the way the markets used to be. I hear stories from a lot of people who'd say, you know, I was trading back then – on October 19, 1987[7] – upstairs in New York and I remember….! Well, I was on the floor of the Board of Trade in Kansas City with a two contract position that I recall went about $275,000 against me – in the worst-case scenario. The truth is, I don't know where I was and I just stopped trading. I couldn't get my prices until late in the day after cutouts.

That was in the good old days of the commodity floor trader, or the specialist post. As traders, you recorded all trades on iPhone-sized trading cards with a number two pencil. Number two pencils also have erasers. In the "good old days" it was not uncommon that money-losing trades would disappear from the trading card of a counterparty. "Oops," they would say, "I don't remember that trade." Or, maybe, "I made it with another guy/gal." So a proprietary trader like me would think I had a good day in the trading pit when, after "cutouts" at the clearing house, I would find an unmatched trade that disappeared.

---

[4] As legally required, the US markets switched from trading in fractional increments to decimal pricing in 2001.

[5] The SEC's Order Handling Rules required market makers (1) to display customer limit orders in their quotes; (2) to display these quotes in the NASDAQ quote montage whenever they have placed more aggressively priced customer quotes in an electronic communications network (ECN); or else, (3) update their own quotes in NASDAQ to match the ECN quotes.

[6] A local in the crowd (local meaning independent of a company) could be registered either as a floor broker, or as a spec trader. Bradley was a spec trader.

[7] This is refers to the day known as Black Monday, when stocks around the world were dumped across markets, erasing a huge value in a short period of trading. The Dow Jones Industrial Average fell 508 points to 1,738.74, or 22.61%.

That's the way we did things back then. Do you want to know why I have been enthusiastic about electronic markets and audit trails? Because I had lived in another world; because I lost a whole lot of money as a young man watching people abuse the system. In the old commodity markets, there were frequent "stop runs"[8] because information about where stops were aggregated in a particular broker's pockets seemed to migrate easily into the crowd. Some locals even used to say, "The customer wants to be stopped in or out of a trade." The abuses then were smaller, I think, because everyone knew where the stops were and positioned themselves accordingly.

Of course, the solution to that abuse was to hold all the stops away from the professionals – out of sight and out of mind. In my mind, the Flash Crash[9] was caused by the solution to a prior problem. The Flash Crash was caused by a massive release of stop orders that became actionable orders when long-term moving average prices were penetrated to the downside.[10]

We had massive electronic stop orders coming out of the brokerage firms and none of the exchanges knew they were coming. Customers tend to place stop loss orders below the 50-day, and the 200-day moving averages, and the retail crowd today behaves like us institutional guys.[11] Electronic brokerage firms allowed retail customers to "stop losses" electronically when the market prices moved below a specified price. Those orders used to sit on the floor in the specialist pocket. They sat packed inside the floor brokers' pockets of their brightly colored vests, on the commodity floors around the country. Those brokers knew what orders were in their pockets – many traded for their own accounts as well. The old boys would wink at their buddies in the crowd. There was a reason people paid tens, and hundreds of thousands of dollars, to be close to the paper in the pit.

---

[8] Stop runs – slang for rapid execution of stop loss orders displayed as printed paper orders and, as Bradley recalled in a follow-up and in his presentation, they were stuffed in floor brokers' jacket pockets. Stop runs were below certain price points on sells; above certain price points on buys. They were entered by brokers on behalf of both commercial trading interests (e.g., grain elevators, exporters, hedge accounts), and speculative trading interests (e.g., retail traders).

[9] Flash Crash of May 6, 2010 lasted about 36 min, erasing 998.5 points in the Dow Jones Industrial Average and then quickly recouped much of the losses as the various indexes rapidly rebounded in this high-speed, electronic-trading phenomenon.

[10] Stop orders become actionable or "live" when the price on the stop loss order is triggered. In a follow-up for this chapter, Bradley explained: "It could be 500 points below the market and they tend to cluster together. In May 2010, this was the first time electronic retail stop orders had been massed near a major market point. When the prices broke down, and through long-term price support points on charts, customer orders that had been "parked" upstairs by the major electronic brokerage houses become live and dumped on an unsuspecting market – causing a massive panic."

Bradley added: "In my days on the floor, some insiders received information about where orders were massed. This was not right for the markets, but the locals then "set up" short trades and covered the shorts on the stop run because they knew ahead of time what the key price levels of the day were."

[11] The markets traded down below the 50-day moving average of prices (a simple average of the close for the most recent 50 trading days), and the 200-day (a simple average of the close for the most recent 200 trading days). There are other averages used – exponential, weighted, and simple stand out – but most trading accounts trading with long-term money use these former as entry and exit points.

Guess what locals did then? We could tell what was about to happen by watching the few guys in the pit who always seemed to be in the know. We sold – shorted futures contracts – a little bit alongside those guys. As prices moved lower, and stops were triggered, the local "shorts" would step in as buyers, cover shorts, and prices almost always bounced significantly in the short run. In the old days, the Chicago Mercantile Exchange and the Kansas City Board of Trade used a practice called "fast markets."[12] That meant the wolves on the floor were eating the lambs – their customers – because sales prices and times were wrong since things were happening so fast. The Flash Crash. Stop runs. Those practices are as old as markets themselves. It just seems worse today because the transparency of electronic markets protects customers from their agents. To me, that's a better market than yesterday for everyone except the owners of trading floor rights.

Now let's talk about the market makers. So I spread traded between Kansas City Value Line Futures and CME S&P Futures. A trader's assistant – call him my good friend, Bob Schwartz – would sit on an open phone to the Chicago floor all day long giving verbal buy and sell orders to a runner on the floor there. Let's say I would buy ten Value Line contracts and immediately ask Bob to sell ten in Chicago. That's until Bob looked at me on October 19th[13] and said I can't get them to answer the phone. They didn't answer the phone on the floor! I was on the floor. I paid a lot of money to be on the floor. And they didn't answer the floor for retail, and they didn't answer the phone for me.

A lot of people cite the Flash Crash as a need to move the markets backward in time – to that good old time of fat market maker margins, to price fixing of spreads on stock trades. So this idea that the market somehow should be returned to the conditions of the "good old days" is bunk. Today, costs are lower, liquidity is higher, and volume is higher.

Guess what? I will tell you what I was doing at the Kaufmann Foundation before I left. I was running $100 million dollars of internally managed money using algorithms provided by Barclays. Do you know what was great about it? I could passively "go along" with trading activity on fairly large orders without impacting price. Algorithms allowed me to trade fairly large blocks of stock. My trading costs were very cheap, very efficient. I found myself in an uncomfortable position, after years

---

[12] Bradley explained in a follow-up that fast markets had everything to do with the state of technology at the time – and the rules that protected the seat holders inside the pits. "When I first started on the floor, prices were recorded by market reporters and transmitted by headset to folks who wrote the most recent price in chalk on the price boards above the trading floor," he said. "Then electronic boards were the big time tech improvement – but prices were viewed by a pit reporter (employed by the exchange) who listened and watched and reported trades as they occurred. When volatility hit the market – trades could be as much as 50 cents or more different on one side of the trading pit from the other."

Bradley added, "The exchange would declare a 'fast market' when the pit recorder couldn't keep up with the bids and asks in the pit – human limitations meant that happened a lot on Black Monday on October 19, 1987. What a fast market implied was that customers would not receive prices anywhere close to what they might have expected in watching the tape of the exchange trades and bids/asks."

[13] Black Monday, see footnote 5.

of advocacy, asking for the public display of all orders so that all market users would benefit from price discovery. Now markets search for liquidity all over the globe. I know I was getting really fair prices on say, my 40,000 share orders on dark pools. Now the questions have to be asked about liquidity versus price. Do prices reflect the equilibrium of supply and demand today? I'm not so sure. More on that later.

Fast forward to 1990 at the TraderForum Annual Conference.[14] I was quoted saying at this conference, "Instinet[15] has become the OTC specialist book." I complained that workstations make market makers vulnerable to predatory moves by competitors. You know what happened back then? Instinet had what was called an I-Only key[16] – where supposed institutions showed orders only to other institutions. NASDAQ responded by launching SelectNet[17] where market makers posted a trading venue exclusively for other market makers. When nominal 1000 share quotes became actionable on SelectNet – that's when the trouble began.

Here's what would happen. I would be trading with, let's pretend, Bill Harts, who represented a large NASDAQ market maker. (Bill, a trading veteran and friend, is here today.) And I would say, "Bill, I am selling XYZ, and I need a bit and I need it fast." Oh, by the way, he didn't know that I had just seen a large institutional seller on Instinet that was displayed only to other institutions. What was supposed to be a feature, to provide anonymity and protection to the buy-side institutional participants, performed

---

[14] TraderForum, part of Institutional Investor, publisher and event organizer, is open to the buy-side only. From its website, this description: "TraderForum, founded in 1984, is the premier invitation-only membership network for equity traders at leading asset management, and hedge fund firms nationwide. Through interactive meetings and conferences and thought-provoking surveys and research studies, trading professionals at more than 165 firms are given invaluable resources to gain a competitive edge in their industry.

[15] Instinet, the institutional, agency-only broker founded in 1967, was one of the earliest off-exchange electronic trading alternatives. Today, it is part of Nomura Group, operating as its independent equity trading unit.

[16] From the website of Themis Trading, this explanation: "I-Only (Q-key) was a mechanism that allowed our institutional and brokerage clients to place larger orders on the system to attract larger contra sides. Orders were placed by institutions and brokers alike with the I-Only attachment that would allow them to be seen by only institutional investors. It was actually routine for institutions and brokers to place I-Only bids and offers on the system for 100,000 shares or more, as they were more confident that leakage and impact would be minimized. Even then we all recognized that there had to be away in the marketplace to allow for larger orders to interact in the marketplace. Even then we knew that a one-size-fits-all market structure couldn't serve the needs of retail investors, retail day traders, institutions, and market makers."

Then came the so-called NASDAQ price-fixing scandal. Explained Themis: "In the wake of the NASDAQ market maker collusion scandal, and recognizing that the markets were becoming faster and more electronic, the SEC implemented Reg ATS. It forced Instinet to abandon the I-Only key and publish its private quotes, in the name of equal and fair access. And so began the movement toward a one-size-fits-all approach to market structure. Since the implementation, markets became faster, and quote and trade sizes shrunk drastically."

For more, see, Themis Trading blog: http://blog.themistrading.com/2014/11/instinet-i-only-equal-acess-bloomberg-tradebook-and-iexs-tops-feed/

[17] Timeline for NASDAQ including enhancements introduced by SelectNet, NASDAQ Timeline: http://www.nasdaq.com/about/timeline.pdf. Source: NASDAQ.

just the opposite function. Institutions compete with each other. They are not friends. So, Bill and other NASDAQ market makers spent more time trying to figure out what they couldn't see, when they were asked to make bids or offers for customers.

I wouldn't even try to talk to the Street. The Street thought I was their enemy because I was an aggressive user of technology – and did not like making block trades with broker capital on the hook. The use of broker capital created all sorts of bad behaviors between market participants, and outright conflicts of interest. Stocks quoted in ½ – that is, 50 cent price – increments would move in multiple price increments when broker capital was involved to facilitate immediate liquidity with little regard for price!

Large mutual funds and other institutional investors complain today when a high-frequency trading firm pays up a penny to access stock for sale in front of big orders. This is an absurd complaint, uninformed by recent history in non-automated markets. I was at the New York Stock Exchange yesterday sitting in the waiting room. On display there is an historic Western Electronic ticker machines once used for price reporting. That was an advantage to being on the exchange back in the day. That is why people paid huge amounts of money to be there.

Access to the floor, historically, provided instantaneous access to information about prices, quantity and trading intentions. The speed of transmission of that information was slow, inaccurate and unreliable. The Internet, high-speed private networks, and the Order Handling Rules,[18] changed the conditions that created stock exchanges. That's a big reason the Big Board demutualized[19]– the value and information advantage gained by standing in the crowd on the NYSE floor was lost. Most members of the exchange were absentee owners and derived high rent incomes from leasing seats to floor traders. The seat values were directly related to profitable trading opportunities afforded to members of the crowd. When trading profits vanished, seat-leasing fees plummeted. Demutualizing allowed members to turn illiquid floor rights into publicly traded claims on the assets of the corporation.

Sorry for the stream of consciousness of my presentation. Bob asked me to relate the last dozen years or so of the changes in micro-market structure. Every story begets another! [laughter]. In any event, my crusade for market structure change was borne from my history as a trader. So here's another story: One day, at American Century, a portfolio manager wandered into the trading room, and said a research analyst had told him that a large West Coast firm had a large block of a particular, small-cap stock for sale. He said we needed to buy this stock. I replied, "Oh really, there aren't any sellers out there." You see, back then the entire industry – from the trading desk to the research salesmen – before transparent, electronic trading finally came about, spent an inordinate amount of time trying to ferret out trading intentions, that is to say, material, non-public information when you get right down to it. It was a fishing expedition, if you will. Now let me pick up the story about the portfolio manager: It was in the period between Christmas and New Year's, when

[18] See, footnote 3.

[19] The New York operated as a mutual organization – non-profit for the benefit of its members – from 1817 until 2006.

the market was quiet, trading was thin. The portfolio manager had walked into our trading room to report this "big buyer" in a thinly traded, small-cap stock. (This kind of information can help out a seller in this stock; it might even indicate that a trader out there had a bad short position after providing capital to a customer.) The portfolio manager rushed over and asked me whether I could sell the stock! I smelled a rat and asked him to have some patience with me. I then called the firm with the "reported" buyer of this stock, saying I heard there was a big seller around and that our portfolio manager was considering his response to this news. Lo and behold, this thinly traded small-cap stock immediately exploded upward in price – by about $3.50 in a matter of a few minutes! The portfolio manager soon realized he had been played. Bad experiences like that at American Century created an understanding of the "sociology of trading." So, not surprisingly, we moved more and more of our trading business onto electronic markets.

I see a lot of people in the back of the room shaking their heads in agreement with me. Okay, it was all about trying to get information about the intentions of people trading, and making money from that. The high-frequency traders settle for fractions of pennies – say .004 pennies a trade, or so it's reported. Thank you, Rich Lindsey, for helping to change that!

Looking at Rich reminds me of another story. I was using Instinet in the late 1990s when I was talking to officials at the SEC under its Chairman Arthur Levitt[20] in regards to the *Market 2000* study. American Century argued that we needed better markets, more transparent markets, and order interaction. I was trading listed stocks on Instinet trying to use ITS.[21] I produced what was called a red book which we took both to the NYSE and to friends at the SEC, to show how many times we were traded around in the marketplace. I presented pages of printed quotes and NYSE trades in Walmart. In fact, there was previous little accountability at the NYSE in the old days. On one of these occasions, I sold 500,000 shares of Walmart in the last 20 min of the trading day. The NYSE specialist quoted the market at ½ bid for 50,000 shares; ¾ offered for 50,000 shares. And I actually sold 500,000 shares at a price of 5/8 in these last 20 min of trading and yet – can you believe it – the quote never changed. The specialist should have narrowed the spread to 1/8 between the bid and the ask; and changed the offer to reflect a 5/8 seller. Exchange officials suggested this could not have happened, and it should not have happened. Yet my experience indicates that such behavior repeated itself every single day back in the day. And that's why specialist firms reported decades of its profitable kind of trading activity – even during the worst disruptions and bear market turbulence. It was this kind of behavior that made the rest of the buy-side community understand that the rules were not followed on the trading floor. The Order Handling Rule followed by Reg NMS[22]

[20] SEC Chairman 1993–2000.

[21] Intermarket Trading System electronically connecting the trading floors of all the major US stock exchanges. Some participants now regard the technology supporting ITS as outdated.

[22] Reg NMS (Regulation National Market System) was adopted by the Securities and Exchange Commission in 2005 and introduced two years later to further advance the ideals of a national market system. The regulation includes the order protection, or trade-through rule, access rule (fair access) to market data including quotations, and rules on sub-penny trading and on market data.

eliminated the very expensive privilege of quoting markets favorable to the interests of the specialists' trading positions.

You want to go back? Let's go back to *Market 2000*. I brought the published report here so everybody could see the sheer volume of this book. It reminds me of when US Representative John Dingell[23] once wrote a letter to Richard Breeden[24] – who preceded SEC Chairman Levitt – demanding answers to market upstarts, such as Instinet that were disruptive to the existing market players. I still remember Dingell's prose when he referred to firms like Instinet as fragmenting, segmenting and balkanizing the nation's stock markets. The best book I read on the NYSE assault on competing technologies over time is Don Weeden's Weeden & Company.[25] Don Weeden wrote about destroying his very own company by doing what was right for markets through the '75 Securities Acts Amendments.[26] Weeden credits the NYSE with replaying the same, anti-competitive rhetoric every time they were competitively threatened.

I have already talked about how only four buy-side firms that authored Comment Letters in response to *Market 2000*. I am told that ours was the only one that was more than two-pages long. We provided transaction cost data, and insight into how stocks traded. We were convinced that electronic trading techniques afforded great protection for the investors in American Century funds and that we had to act to defend these nascent innovators and disrupters in the nation's securities markets. Bill Lyons, our General Council, who then became the President of American Century, insisted that we fly to Washington, DC., to sit down with the authors of the report. We sat down with a young regulator, Janet Angstadt, who is here today, and with Howard Kramer, to talk about this because we were using electronic trading technology with great effort for our investors. We thought that the whole political pall over *Market 2000* was aiming to undermine new systems with archaic rules. So imagine our surprise when these really smart staffers had the courage to offer data-driven insight and analysis, and a clear vision of the future of markets.

By the way, almost everything that we have experienced over the last 20 years was laid out in that 1994 document in *Market 2000*. It was a blueprint for regulation and rulemaking – and not many people read it. I read the whole thing – mostly looking for footnotes citing our comment letter, I admit, but I read it. Very few other people did.

I actually met Bob Schwartz for the first time during the comment gathering period by the SEC for *Market 2000*. Bob was invited to talk about market structure to a committee of ICI[27] members in Washington, DC. That meeting was my first

[23] The Michigan Democrat did not seek reelection and retired from Congress on January 2015.

[24] SEC Chairman 1989–1993.

[25] Weeden & Co. The New York Stock Exchange and the Struggle over a National Securities Market. Donald E. Weeden. (2002). Donald Weeden is on the Board of Directors of Weeden & Co., having previously served as its Chairman.

[26] Landmark legislation that fostered the creation of a national market system alongside a system for nationwide clearing and settlement of securities transactions. The law ushered in the abolition of fixed commissions.

[27] The Investment Company Institute is the nationwide association of US investment companies.

exposure to the practice of the trade – where portfolio managers and traders are insulated from discussions about rules pertaining to portfolio management and trading. Lawyers, with no requisite skills or experience, sit quietly in rooms listening to experts, and then pen a response that the interest group tells them is appropriate. The traders are also prisoners of what is called soft-dollar commitments – the use of trading commissions to pay the costs of technology and of research.

Most institutional asset managers historically did not view trading as an important professional job. Buy-side traders were often recruited from the back office, or from portfolio accounting, and were asked to oversee the transfer of their client's transmissions to pay the bills of the firm. Over the past five years, trading volumes fell, market speed increased, technology costs expanded for the buy-side – and yet many traders engage in histrionics about decimal trading and high-frequency traders. Why? Because trading is more difficult, cents per share have collapsed, and the management company still gives traders the same bills to pay.

Traders should get upset when their hands are tied. Let me briefly digress. Wall Street just invented another trading commission workaround called a Commission Sharing Agreement – or CSA, a form of what were once called soft dollars. Some things remain the same today. CSAs start with an operating assumption that most soft-dollar converters, or investment research boutiques, have inadequate traders and trading technology. So, the SEC decided it was OK for traders to select one execution broker who could then pay all of an investment manager's research chits, instead of allocating trades to 15 or more brokers with inferior trade execution abilities. Yet nobody in the regulatory infrastructure dares take on the sacred cow of soft dollars. The use of commissions to pay for research was borne during the era of fixed commissions, and perpetuated by the 28(e) Safe Harbor in the 1975 Amendment to the Securities Exchange Act.[28] Soft dollars are anachronistic. Arthur Levitt, along with Rich Lindsey when he was at the SEC, tried to create accountability several times around the use of soft dollars. They went after internalization several times, and they couldn't get it done because of institutional resistance and Wall Street protectors in Congress. (In any event, I wrote in my *Market 2000* brief that, if we went to decimals, we would wipe out payment for order flow. I never could have dreamed that we would start rebating tape revenues.[29])

Let's pick up the story at Twentieth Century back in the mid-1990s, when we were trading hundreds of millions of shares electronically. I invited the SEC staff to watch us trade, and one day in particular – and it may have been when Annette Nazareth[30] was the Director of Market Regulation – SEC regulators heard frequent whining from the Wall Street crowd that difficult orders could not be traded electronically – that you needed market makers and human interaction to grease the

---

[28] See, footnote 18.

[29] This gained ground as ATSs and execution venues ratcheted up the pressure competing for liquidity.

[30] Nazareth served at the SEC from 1998 to 2008.

wheels of trade. With several staff members standing in our trading room, we received an order to sell two million shares of Dell. Not only did regulators hear that trading small stocks was not possible on these venues, they were regularly being told that big orders could not be traded because of small visible order sizes. I remember telling the regulators about this Dell order, and asked them to watch how we would aggressively sell the ticket late in the trading day. I had three traders, and asked them to each hit every venue. We sold all the stock within a quarter point in about 10 min – and then the stock moved lower. Seeing is believing, but we did get a little lucky on that particular day with market regulators gathered in our trading room who were eager to rebut anecdotal whining by the low-tech, marginal market players.

What was more important to the regulators was the average trade size on that two-million share order. When we first began trading large orders on Instinet, the accounting was extremely difficult. [Bradley holds aloft yellow notepad.] My traders and I recorded each small lot traded on big orders, and tried to keep running totals all day so that we didn't overshoot an order.

I was writing down our average trade size. It was like 1230 shares. People didn't trade blocks on networks. Everyone pinged everybody else. So I would do 41 trades of 1200 shares – to trade a 100,000 share ticket. The more we traded in this manner, the lower were our reported trading costs. The manual task of trade reporting taxed the early adopters of these technologies.

The answer to this vexing problem was FIX.[31] Is everyone here familiar with FIX? That wasn't easy. Pete Jenkins, my friend and buy-side trading professional (in the audience), worked with me on all of these initiatives back in the 90s. One day he called me up and said, did you hear about this committee being put together, it is called the Financial Information Exchange? Because back then the brokers wanted to own the protocol.

Fidelity's buy-side desk started the protocol, and hoped to establish the equivalent of an "open source" collaborative effort among buy-side and sell-side firms – to establish a software protocol to identify trading terms, order types, currency and clearing functions so that all trading counterparties could communicate securely and effectively. Scott Atwell at American Century is still in charge of the technical spec committee today. I was on the original executive committee. American Century and Putnam Investments were among the thought leaders, in forcing brokerage firms representing our interests to be compliant with the FIX protocol. Scott wrote the FIX protocol for us and assisted several of our brokers. What did FIX do? In my opinion it was more important than decimals. FIX gave us a standard language so that when the Order Handling Rules went into place in 1997, the Instinet highway proved inadequate for the huge jump in quote traffic and it was crushed. Instinet started shutting off certain trade-related information to preserve bandwidth, and negotiation and trade information slowed.

[31] The Financial Information eXchange (FIX) protocol is the electronic communications protocol introduced in 1992 for real-time exchange of trading information in securities transaction.

I stood up in our trading room and said that it was time to switch. We had Bloomberg and Archipelago alternative trading systems enabled on our trading platform. But I was reluctant to switch from a platform that had served our investors so well. I didn't think I was ready to do it, I was still a little chicken. But real slowness, not the crybaby slowness cited by those who complain about paying for co-location and microsecond advantage,[32] made me swallow my fears and hit the button to light up the new platforms on our trading desk.

Within one week, we shifted almost the entirety of our enormous electronic trading business to emerging competitors, Archipelago and Bloomberg's B-Trade.[33] Stories have been repeated to me that the SEC made calls to both of these platforms, wanting to know the reason for the enormous volume increases. So FIX, along with prudent SEC regulation, through the promulgation of the Order Handling Rules, created a marketplace that surveys showed the buy-side had long demanded – transparent, anonymous, and electronic. From this point forward, we saw the increasing algorithm war games play out as each of the competitors tried to replicate human behavior by allowing traders to choose an algorithm that fit their trading style.

This napkin (Bradley holds up a cloth napkin) represents one from a dinner I had with Rich Lindsey, along with Carrie Dwyer and Mark Tellini who were all senior advisors for SEC Chairman Arthur Levitt. They were interested in ways to create more competitive and more transparent markets. And we were talking about how markets could be improved. I provided print-outs of market maker quotes and trades that my firm made through the quotes – we locked and crossed the market in the lingo of the trade. I explained that I couldn't get market makers to move, and I couldn't get them to trade. Oftentimes, the market maker refused to move an offer in the old days, not because the market maker was an actual seller of the stock, but because he or she was short the stock and trying to influence trading in the stock. Remember, prior to the Order Handling Rules, the quotes from the institutional trader were not incorporated into the public quote. Some Wall Street traders would stand on the quote, until they received a phone call from the management company trying to buy or sell stock. The price of information was far more valuable than the trading such firms endured from so-called SOES bandits.[34]

I had discussions with trading partners, such as Morgan Stanley, who moved the Instinet machine from their trading floor so they couldn't say they were not honoring those quotes prior to the Order Handling Rules. By the way, at the New York Stock Exchange, floor trader, Billy Johnson,[35] was the only one on the floor allowed

---

[32] Refers here to the much debated practice of "co-location" by high-frequency trading, or HFT firms, of their computerized boxes next to an exchange server, placed there for the advantage of split second price trading data feeds. Most investors, by contrast, get their price data feeds slightly later through consolidated prices through the market. The New York Stock Exchange, indeed, has made substantial revenue from co-location services.

[33] These operated as Electronic Communications Networks.

[34] Day traders, who used NASDAQ's Small Order Execution System (SOES), were accused by NASDAQ market makers of "picking off" their stale quotes that hadn't been refreshed in these earliest of high-speed markets. Market makers branded these days traders, "SOES Bandits."

[35] Billy Johnson served as exchange president from 1996 to 2002.

to retain an Instinet machine. Billy shared with me that then NYSE Chairman and CEO, Dick Grasso, banned the machine from the floor. I don't know how Billy defied the ban, but he did it at NYSE specialist firm LaBranche, prior to Billy's ascendency to the NYSE presidency. So basically, here's the bottom line – we shouldn't go back to the way things used to be.

The regulators, through the *Market 2000* process, in about 1994, prescribed the transparent markets we have today. This is what Janet and colleagues wrote here (holding up *Market 2000* study). We can improve transparency by displaying limit orders. Why was everybody acting like the Commissions' action on the Order Handling Rules in 1997 was such a surprise? After the Order Handling Rules, it took until 2001 to eliminate the 1/8th pricing system that provided a wealth transfer function from individual investors to Wall Street market makers. You may recall that NASDAQ counter-acted the success of Instinet with transparent orders, and electronically accessible markets with its own version, called SelectNet. SelectNet was a market maker "only" quoted market with better prices than those offered to the public – prior to the Order Handling Rules. Yet the brokers continued to work around the display rules, using technicalities and the timidity of the SEC who fears confronting the Street. If you want to look today at the dark pools that are owned by the broker dealers, they are immensely bigger than what NASDAQ's SelectNet or Instinet I-Only[36] represented at the time. How in the world have they escaped any of the transparency rules that were implied in these rules?

So why did Bob Schwartz invite me here to speak? We share much history. I just left the Kauffman Foundation and may be retiring from the business, after almost 20 years fighting in the trenches of micro-market structure. I have worked closely with kindred spirits on the buy-side in New York City. Prior to the early 1990s, the buy-side was notoriously silent on issues pertaining to the ways markets worked. We were supposed to hire brokers to do our bidding, and to send along sufficient commission streams to pay for research and technology and "stuff," and not ask too many questions. My kindred spirits were buy-side traders Pete [Jenkins], Holly Stark, Mike Murphy and I – before Mike suffered sell-side recidivism when he moved to the sell-side. Holly and Mike both had worked for smaller firms. Peter and I represented partnership interests and family ownership at the time. We were generally unencumbered by the political niceties of the business; a self-regulatory-organization, or SRO, did not regulate our companies. The four of us spent years organizing and presenting an extremely well-attended "Institutional Tuesday" program on the last morning of the national Security Traders Association (STA) annual meeting – where market structure experts such as Benn Steil and Bob Schwartz were our guests and commentators. Our stridency earned us an invitation out of the group, when our notorious "Gang of Four" amped up our criticism of institutional trading practices. When that happened, we found a home with the Investment Company Institute, and helped Ari Burstein of ICI launch the trading committee there – giving the buy-side a strong voice for the first time on 1933–1934 Act issues.

[36]A mechanism that permitted institutional and brokerage clients to place larger orders on the system to lure larger contra sides.

To be sure, the vested interests on Wall Street yearn for and advocate return to the "good old days." But do people remember what happened to the 24 firms that paid $925 million and NASDAQ who paid $875,000, for failure to supervise market-making practices?[37] I recall one of my institutional presentations to the STA entitled, "Practices that Poison Trust." I talked about a variety of conventions used by traders on both sides of the Street. I challenged adherence to the rules, and laid out specific examples of what were dishonest trading practices – such as not reporting trades in a timely fashion to the tape. One of the old market maker "deans" sprang to his feet in the middle of my talk, and yelled out that his firm would lose a lot of money if they followed the rules as the SEC prescribed. This occurred the same week that the Justice Department had initiated an investigation into NASDAQ trading practices – and we later learned a Justice Department representative was in that very audience to become better immersed in the culture of trading.

Moving on from that era and radical change to markets ushered in by the Order Handling Rules, we arrive at 1999. The World Wide Web was just being rolled out. Regulation Fair Disclosure (Reg FD)[38] was one of the earliest recognitions that all investors and analysts enjoyed unlimited and unprecedented access to company executives, whose quarterly conference calls expounded on trends, risks and opportunities for the company's business. When phone lines into a central point were scarce, the broker served to talk to companies and transmit information to valued clients – ever heard of the "First Call"? That company tried to supplant the brokers who often promised the "First Call" on company news to favorite commission-paying clients. Reg FD recognized that payment for access to market-moving information was closely related to insider trading activities. Arthur Levitt and his staff at the SEC anticipated much of the evolution in our markets – and with innovative rule making encouraged companies to use Internet communication to release information to all market participants at the same time. This was then really radical stuff.

Let's talk about decimals. There was incredible opposition to ideas that our stock prices should be priced in decimals. The elocution about positive "externalities" related to wide market spreads continues through today. The move to decimals was a common sense act – as Instinet, Bloomberg and other emerging automated trading systems allowed hedge funds to split the eighth ad infinitum. Hedge funds required an uptick to short a stock. The rule didn't say a 1/8th of a dollar uptick – so hedge funds started shorting stocks up 1/16th, then 1/32rd. Competitors decided splitting prices was a competitive strategy and, finally, Instinet offered 1/256th cent splits. I testified with Peter in front of Congress in favor of decimal pricing. In my testimony, I held up large plastic cards distributed by Herzog Heine Geduld and other NASDAQ market makers, with easy to see conversions from fractions to decimals. I always thought that having the market display prices in that matter was much better than figuring out where to hang dirty, tattered plastic cards near the trading terminals.

[37] On July 17, 1996, the US Justice Department charged the biggest houses on Wall Street – firms like Merrill Lynch, JPMorgan and predecessor firms to Citigroup – with price fixing and collusion on NASDAQ.

[38] Approved by the SEC on August 15, 2000.

Bob Schwartz, Benn Steil (a long-time colleague and collaborator with Bob) and I traveled to Europe in the early days of the automation of the European stock trading systems. Subsequently, Benn spent years at the Royal Institute of Financial Affairs focused on market microstructure there. When he returned to the States, he and Ian Domowitz published "Automation, Trading Costs and Structure of the Securities Trading Industry"[39] (Bradley holds it up). It was a seminal paper, using more than a decade's data on trading costs attributable to market makers, brokers, and automated trading systems. For years, folks speculated that the data must have belonged to Fidelity Investments. I will reveal today that the data was mine. I asked them not to reveal our identity in the paper. But I was anxious for independent validation of the data that I had shared with regulators, and the Street for many years, that demonstrated enormous cost savings that I think was attributable to our anonymity in the marketplace.

And my last physical exhibit for my talk is this little report put together by Steve Galbraith at Bernstein Research in the late 1990s. Perhaps I liked the report so much because he cited much of my work at the time. He analyzed enormous changes in the market's payment structures and made bold predictions of imminent change. The report was courageous and controversial and absolutely prescient. (Reading from the report): "Declining trading costs, combined with structural inefficiencies at the exchanges, have resulted in unsustainable quasi-monopolistic returns for participants in the trading chain. A window is open for the creation of a major alternative to the NASDAQ and NYSE; existing exchange players could see current returns halved." None of the changes in this market – research, automated trading, decimals – should have been a surprise. I think the real surprise to the Wall Street executives was how fast the political support system collapsed that protected the "old way."

Now fast forward to today. The regulators have become essentially referees at a rugby scrum. They have refused to deal with non-disclosed, not transparent actionable orders in dark pools. And folks in corporate finance avoid confrontation with investment banks on changing the incredible bureaucracy around Initial Public Offerings (IPOs). At American Century, I enjoyed a period of years where the company financed our "bets" on disruptive technologies that would make Wall Street more accountable – with names like Open IPO, Archipelago, and on the research side, StarMine. I am still a believer that we need to do something with the placement of "hot" IPOs in the market, and I am a huge advocate for Bill Hambrecht's Open IPO process despite the array of vested interests – the largest VC fund partnerships and partners, investment banks, hedge funds – whose control of underwriting and distribution create enormous artificial spreads for the activity. IPOs are priced and traded today like they were 20 years ago. Where else have such profit margins survived without the help of a meddling regulatory protector?

[39] Automation, Trading Costs and Structure of the Securities Trading Industry (1997). Ian Domowitz and Benn Steil. Department of Economics and Institute for Policy Research, Northwestern University, and International Economics Programme, the Royal Institute of International Affairs, respectively, at the time.

Finally, I want to talk about the notion of a market maker's affirmative obligations. Regulators and academics often counsel the imposition of affirmative obligations on trading partners. With the idea being that market makers enjoy special benefits – "easy profits" – during calm market environments that will be paid back many times over, during adverse market environments when they would be compelled by rule to take the other side of trades. As the system was collapsing under the weight of new, high-speed technologies and SEC and Justice Department actions, many opined that affirmative obligations could better protect the public during events like those in 2008 and 2009. In behavioral finance terms, this could be characterized as a narrative fallacy. The same idea gets reported many times over many eras and many years, becoming received wisdom with absolutely no supporting data. It was argued that a specialist would make money most of the time – but then provide significant excess capital when the markets needed the money during periods of high stress.

I yearned for convincing data to prove to me that at some point over the last 50 years, specialists, or market makers, actually acted with altruistic notions to provide more capital during those scary times. I finally got it from Mike LaBranche of LaBranche, when he was doing a road show for LaBranche before his specialist firm took the company public. He asked for a meeting with me at American Century – I thought the business was doomed and didn't want to own a specialist firm – but I accepted the meeting. Mike said during the meeting that he was there to convince me of the strong underlying economics of trading firms, and why it merited my consideration as an investor. Now this was years ago, and my recollection might be imperfect, but it is generally correct that the LaBranche IPO pitch book had a long history of what he termed the "principal realization rate."

Michael represented that NYSE specialist firm LaBranche. This specialist firm enjoyed profitability every quarter for 22 years; including the period of the market's single biggest one-day drop in 1987, and also during major bear markets in 1980 and 1982, and in other periods of market distress. The data were quite compelling in support of the business of market making as a specialist, and still more compelling in support of the notion that any justification of special trading privileges in exchange for affirmative obligations in the market was unsupported by any real world experience.

But, before you ask me any questions, let me talk briefly about this so-called endangered species, the cash equities marketplace. You may think that exchanges are endangered species. It may be that we are worried about regulation and the options market, about how we are going to converge or harmonize regulation from futures to options, and cash equities to this and that, and that we are confronted with potential events like the Flash Crash. That's not what I am worried about. Let's talk about who's really whining the most today. The largest traders, and now hedge funds too. It's amazing when all the big boys start to whine.

Hedge funds and big institutional firms, insurance companies, pension funds, and the mutual funds are all whining and demanding regulatory relief from annoying, high-frequency traders! They are whining because they think some little motor boat is racing in front of their huge cruise liner, and trading in front of them. You know what? The analysis is not wrong. Because most of them are paying bills, and are so ham handed and clumsy with algorithms that they sit there and do the same thing day after day, hour after hour, minute after minute, and then expect people to stand down so that they can trade a big block. Guess what? There is no economic law anywhere that suggests big blocks should be immune from moving the market. Either institutional traders should get smarter about how to use algos, or their firms should shrink their size. The only rule in finance is that the bigger a fund's assets, the bigger the footprint in the market.

Where in the world did they teach in a finance class that the bigger you get the cheaper things should be? Oh, that is called economies of scale (wink). I argue that economies of scale extend well to the management companies, but they sure don't apply to huge piles of money in a single fund, or management company. Enormous concentration of assets in a single strategy or strategies, necessitate enormous stock ownership positions that can take weeks, and sometimes months, to accumulate or distribute in the marketplace. Big blocks don't enjoy lower costs. They should be more expensive. After all, the Street and market makers, skated in front of these orders in the dark for decades.

Now that such orders are lit up on trading screens for everyone to see, the behaviors are the same, the spreads are much smaller, and the overall costs are a fraction of what they were before any of the data are to be believed. The only things that scales with big assets under management are the profits to the management firm, and the fees to the hedge fund. Small traders are going to eat their lunch (and should); until investors move to smaller funds and more nimble managers for better investment returns.

When I left for Kauffman, I had a team of ten people at American Century we called "American Century Tomorrow," with a two-million-dollar budget for engineers, quantitative engineers, software engineers and historical price databases. Fast forward five years, and I performed the same analytical work in my new home with a quantitative engineer and a software engineer. Our extensive Thomson Reuters data feed with micro data cost me about $280,000 per year, and I had a contract with a cloud computing firm in Seattle for $36,000 a year. They gave me the same computing power, and vastly more for about 10% of what the same infrastructure required less than ten years earlier.

Processing speed has increased exponentially. Costs for data and systems have plummeted. High-frequency traders represent adaptable, aggressive providers of micro liquidity to the market. Given the collapse in costs and the increase in transparency and market access today, I would far rather be running a firm with $20 million or $30 million, skating around these big orders, because they are really easy to see – and there is no way to hide them.

When I started in the business, it took one and half days for an institutional firm to trade an average-size order. Plexus data suggested that most traders limited daily trading to less than 20% of daily trading volume. I could never figure out why trading volume didn't just expand overall because the average days to work an order in the market was several – not one. Why was trading so parsed into the markets of yesterday? The buy-side feared the exchanges. The buy-side feared the brokers. The buy-side had research obligations to pay with soft-dollar commissions. The buy-side failed to invest in the necessary technology. But there is so much fear out there – the more an order stretches out in time, the easier it is to game. What does that mean for small companies where liquidity has been a challenge from the 60s to the 80s, and through this decade? I argue that it is high time for exchange-sponsored call auctions for small and mid-cap stocks where continuous market trading environments – and well-founded fears and risk – conspire to keep buyers and sellers of securities temporarily distant. I can't even fathom that regulators still afford any respect to the idea that we should widen the spread and give research incentives to brokerage firms.! Do we have any questions?

Bill Harts Harold, you published with Robert Litan a paper about ETFs and the cost of listing in 2010.[40] Has anything changed since then?

Bradley I always have to backtrack a bit into history before moving forward. Hugh Quigley ran the Merrill Lynch trading desk in the late 1980s, and invited two young traders named [Pete] Jenkins and [Harold] Bradley to talk about how the buy-side was changing. He shared with us that Merrill made 4½ cents a share, I think, every time they touched a NASDAQ order. That's why they could afford to pay a penny per share for order flow from customers. This was a practice originally begun by Bernard Madoff back in the 1970s and 1980s. That 4½ cents represented the average profit margin available to market makers for ever share traded.

Today, the HFT guys, performing the same function, make about 7/100 cents share for every share traded. In 1992, the average cost of trading a $20 stock on NASDAQ – this is from my old trading data from American Century – was 23 cents a share. In the fourth quarter of 2009, shortly after one of the most tumultuous environments in trading history, the implicit and explicit trading costs of an order were about 10 cents a share, according to ITG. Why is this relevant to Bill's question?

Bob Litan and I published our paper in 2010, and analyzed the components of the Flash Crash. Bob is formerly a "thinker" at the Brookings Institute, and now he's chief economist at Bloomberg. We saw demonstrable problems with the trading impact of unsettled trades in ETFs, linkages between ETFs and derivatives and cash securities. We saw historically unprecedented correlations between individual stocks and "the market."

Our thesis became that the collapse in single stock trading spreads had infused the massive growth in ETF trading, where market makers could create and trade much more complex instruments, outside of cash equities, in the search for sustainable market maker profits. Bob Litan and I concluded that electronic markets were not to blame, and that the smoking gun for the Flash Crash existed in the largely unregulated market-making environment between cash equities, indexes, futures and ETFs.

---

[40] Choking the Recovery: Why New Growth Companies Aren't Going Public and Unrecognized Risks of Future Market Disruption. Harold Bradley and Robert E. Litan. November 8, 2010. Ewing Mario Kauffman Foundation. http://www.etf.com/docs/KauffmanETF_Report_I.pdf?iu=1

I spent a good week reading prospectuses trying to figure out how market makers – called Associated Parties – are compelled to create or destroy ETFs. By rule, I can't get a good definition anywhere. We attributed the Flash Crash to the collapse first, in small company ETFs that migrated electronically and instantly to large company ETFs, then to indexes and then to stocks. The data seemed to support the idea that the tail was wagging the dog. And arbitrage didn't work in the transference from apparently liquid packages to illiquid individual securities, contained within those packages.

When you are looking at a large institutional portfolio you want diversification. You get diversification by investing across different sectors, in different companies. Right? Who learned that in finance? ETFs have fostered an environment where allocation by hedge funds and others has enormous tax-escape advantages, and may be undermining capital allocation to efficient managers of specific companies.

The old saw is that in a market crisis correlations rise to 1 – meaning that prices for all securities move in the same direction and to the same degree. A JPMorgan unit published charts that were used in our paper that illustrated this disturbing and increasing trend for small stocks, for all stocks, to move together in statistical lockstep that before had only occurred during severe market stress. Three months ago, the dollars traded in the SPY, the so-called Spyder ETF, exceeded the dollars traded in all underlying securities in the S&P 500. When the derivatives are driving price formation, you are not discovering price. We published the data, our analysis and our theory, two years ago, and we remain confident in our analysis, despite the ad hominem attacks that occurred after we published our concerns.

Bill, I think the SEC is terrified to touch the regulation of ETFs. ETFs are created at astonishing speed and sold as being "liquid," despite often being crammed full of illiquid securities. The SEC doesn't want to touch the ETF market because it has become the most profitable engine of growth on Wall Street now. And I will go one step further. Bill and I debated this a little at an earlier time. Securities lending is all messed up, and it is concentrated among five or six firms in a major and systemic risky way – and it ties right into ETFs. This paper, "Choking the Recovery," is available online.

Thank you.

Robert Schwartz Harold, this mike is still smoking. You can see why I have a lot of Harold stories, but he tells them better than me.

[Applause]

Chapter 6
New Initiators: Technology, Market Events, and Business Practices

Brett Redfearn, Kevin Callahan, George Kledaras, Timothy J. Mahoney, Joseph M. Mecane, and Joe Ratterman

Brett Redfearn It is my great pleasure to engage a group as well-informed about market structure as this panel. For one thing, this concept of new initiators is frequently discussed. We have had many in-depth industry discussions lately about market structure. So I really love Bob Schwartz's idea of focusing on a targeted theme, which today at this conference is specifically about innovation and change, the special things our industry is attempting to achieve as it strives to make better markets.

It seems there is a clamor to ease off the changes – and to back off from some of the innovation. There are debates about too much fragmentation; too much competition; too much speed; too many order types. Should we ban order types? Should we slow our markets down? We obviously have a very complicated and interesting

B. Redfearn (✉)
J.P. Morgan Securities, New York, NY, USA

K. Callahan
AX Trading Network, New York, NY, USA

G. Kledaras
FIX Flyer, New York, NY, USA

T.J. Mahoney
BIDS Trading L.P., New York, NY, USA

J.M. Mecane
NYSE, New York, NY, USA

J. Ratterman
BATS Global Markets, Inc., Kansas City, MO, USA

R.A. Schwartz et al. (eds.), *Rapidly Changing Securities Markets*, Zicklin School of Business Financial Markets Series,
DOI 10.1007/978-3-319-54588-2_6

market structure. Nonetheless, there is the question of whether or not such changes would impede innovation? With that as a backdrop, let's start down the line, first with Kevin, and then continue with each panelist explaining his firm's particular innovation.

Kevin Callahan AX Trading Network has introduced a trader-initiated call auction. We are an alternative trading system, or ATS, with a crossing system that enables any trader to start their own auction in any stock at any time. Call auctions, of course, are not all that innovative, they have been here a long time.

In fact, long before we had formal stock exchanges – back when stocks traded at coffee houses and pubs – stocks changed hands via a trader-initiated call auction. You literally called an auctioneer and said, for example, I want to sell some stock, say the equivalent of Bank of America shares today, and the auctioneer spread the word out. So, by the following Wednesday at the coffee house, an auction took place for your stock. In many ways what we are doing today is actually innovative. But, in some other ways, it is going back 200 years to the days of a coffee house, albeit in a virtual environment. We haven't figured out yet how to serve beer or coffee over the Internet, but we are working on that! [laughter]

George Kledaras FIX Flyer is a software infrastructure company that provides a lot of the base core for order routing technology, from the network all the way up to sophisticated software into risk controls. We are providing a lot of high-speed services. In our view, the two major trends over the last couple of years are the large growth in direct market access (DMA)[1] and in algorithmic support to markets globally.

Everybody wants to have faster markets, either locally or from, let's say, North America or Europe, right out to emerging markets. Here's another trend. We have had the largest mutual funds in the USA completely upgrading their infrastructure to very low latencies to enable them to start rolling out their own algos. They're always trying to reduce costs in their system.

Timothy J. Mahoney Here are two innovative things at BIDS. First, we formed a venue to trade blocks with buy-side manual users and sell-side algorithms. It may seem simple, but it had not been done before. We think it has added to the liquidity of the system. Second, we have embraced collaboration. I would argue that the great innovators of the late twentieth century were sitting alone in their garages hooking up a great idea and then taking it to market by themselves. The great innovation of the twenty-first century will occur in problem-solving collaboration between corporations and companies. Here are two good examples. The first brings in my friend Joe Mecane of the New York Stock Exchange. We have put together the New York Block Exchange in a way that tries to combine the lit market and dark crossing.[2]

[1] Direct market access describes direct electronic access for buy-side firms to the order books of exchanges.

[2] By early 2013, the NYSE and BIDS joint venture for block trades was coming to an end. See NYSE and BIDS to end block trading joint venture. John McCrank, *Reuters*, February 8, 2013. http://www.reuters.com/article/2013/02/08/us-nyse-bids-idUSBRE9170ZC20130208

The second example is our collaboration with Bloomberg.[3] And we have formed partnerships that have enabled the participants to have most of the benefits of an internal crossing engine without creating another venue.

Joe Mecane Our markets have become too complicated. However, I disagree a bit on this complete notion of complexity. I don't think we can look at all the complaints about market structure in terms of order types, or high-frequency trading. You have to trace it back to the underlying market structure problems people are trying to solve. One of the more innovate things we have at the NYSE is our Retail Liquidity Program,[4] a program that benefits retail customers. It is a new concept for exchanges. But it is not a new concept for the marketplace. Of course, the changes we are all making certainly add to the overall market complexity.

Joe Ratterman BATS operates exchanges both in the USA and in Europe. We have two US exchanges that together have about a 13% market share.[5] In Europe we are the largest stock exchange with 25% market share in equity trading. We have another market for options which is about 3.5% to 4%.[6] With our innovations the past 2 years, we have been looking for ways to incent behavior that creates a better experience for people coming to trade in the market. The first we call National Best Bid and Offer (NBBO) Setter.[7] It was looking at the behavior we wanted to promote – market makers that posted quotes to move the market forward, to improve the best bid or best offer on our market. In this case we provide an incremental incentive in the rebate program for those orders – that basically moved the bid up or the offer down. And we created a better price for those coming into the market afterwards. We have since applied that to our equities markets as well.

The second major innovation is in market making.[8] Once again, the idea is to look for that specific behavior – and for market makers competing for the best possible displayed market on a competitive basis. The traditional market making programs typically have a designation associated with them. That means that somebody is designated as the market maker for a security. They may have a few minimal

[3]This program, BPool, was announced in early 2012 as an effort of BIDS Trading and Bloomberg to assist the buy side and sell side in trading blocks.

[4]New York Stock Exchange's Retail Liquidity Program (RLP) was approved earlier in 2012 by the Securities and Exchange Commission. As of writing, the RLP permits market makers to offer stock prices for retail investors at fractions of a penny superior than the prevailing market rate. The program, reflecting how dark pools and wholesalers operate, is aimed at luring order flow back to NYSE. As of writing in summer 2015, the program was reporting a minimum weekly volume – executing 2.5 million shares on one specific week – with one analyst describing the RLP as "unsuccessful."

[5]As of writing in 2015, BATS operated four US exchanges and reported a market share of 21% of equity trading volume.

[6]As of writing in 2015, BATS reported a market share of 10%.

[7]This press release explains the concept in more detail. BATS OPTIONS Unveils NBBO Setter Rebates. December 13, 2010. http://www.businesswire.com/news/home/20101213005961/en/BATS-Options-Unveils-NBBO-Setter-Rebates#.VYq6jVKYFrY

[8]For additional explanation, see BATS website https://www.batstrading.com/listings/market_maker/etp/

obligations, and they have the benefits of being that designee. Our competitive program allows sponsored market makers to compete on a second-by-second basis for the best price and the most size at the best price. So 23,400 times a day – which is the number of seconds in the trading day – we take a snapshot of which market maker is performing the best in terms of a reference market. We then award them the winning assignment for that second. Whoever provides the most consistent performance over the entire day receives the daily award as market maker of the day.[9] The focus is on quoting behavior, applied in a way that will be potentially highlighted on some illiquid securities, such as ETFs. It is also applied in a way that motivates behavior that you want. And that is better priced orders sitting in the market as a reference price for others to come and trade with.

Redfearn And, typically, for less active securities in the program?

Ratterman Absolutely.

Redfearn Perhaps there is just a bit too much complexity? At the same time, there is a lot of innovation. Speed cannot just be through high-frequency traders. Trading speeds measured in microseconds also exist for institutional traders. What about client segmentation? We all remember when each exchange would have the same price, same deal, and same trading program for all of its customers.[10] We are now talking about changing that a bit, and of allowing different ways for segmenting the market within exchanges for different types of market participants.

So let's start with the issue of client segmentation because this was a hotly debated issue around NYSE's RLP Program for the retail market. The RLP rule filing was quickly approved, and it is now live in the market. We are moving away from a period where we expect that exchanges should have the same rules for everybody, and into a world where – because of internalization and what is happening at various brokers – the exchanges now have to say, "Okay, we now have one special carve out deal for our retail customers, and another special deal for institutional traders," or something along those lines? Is this a trend? Kevin, how do you look at segmentation? It seems to be the core of what you offer.

---

[9] The winning assignment means they are considered the firm that was at the inside of the bid-ask spread during that particular second. If the firm wins more assignments than anyone over the course of the day, then they receive the CLP, or Competitive Liquidity Provider, reward for that day. As of writing, the CLP program would expire July 28, 2015, unless extended.

The program worked like this, according to BATS' website: "Each day CLPs compete for a reward ranging from $20 to $400. The reward is split between the top two CLPs on the bid side and the offer side. The top two CLPs on each side receive 60% and 40% of their side's split, respectively. For example, if the daily reward for an ETP is $200, $100 is awarded to the top two CLPs on the bid side, and $100 is awarded to the top two CLPs on the offer side — $60 going to the first-place CLP, and $20 going to the second-place CLP."

"To become one of the top two CLPs, Market Makers are awarded 'credits' for winning SETs (Size Event Tests) during the trading day. A SET is a random testing event done within each second between 9:25 a.m. and 4:05 p.m. ET."

[10] See footnote 3.

Callahan It is at the very core of what we are offering; it very much replicates the behavior of the upstairs trading world. We are trying to transform some of that upstairs liquidity into an electronic exchange-like environment. Segmentation is a big issue in the institutional marketplace.

We are talking about clients calling up brokers saying, "Listen I want to do something in a name, make some calls, call the top holders; maybe I want to trade only with long-only investors." Buy-side traders want to control how their trading information is being used and who is seeing that information. We give them the ability to do that. Our platform allows the buy-side trader to control who gets invited to the auction. To promote market fairness, however, we also protect all resting orders in the system. All resting orders, no matter where they come from, get swept into the auction.

Redfearn Can I go into the system and say that I want to trade with this specific group of people? If somebody comes in who is not on my list, is it the case that they can't trade?

Callahan You can control who sees your information and who gets invited. But we do protect those orders that are resting in the system.

Redfearn George, are you seeing anything like this?

Kledaras This is more of a higher level thing for us. I can tell you this much – everybody pays attention to the FIX Protocol[11] because it enables them to access all these things much more seamlessly.

Mahoney Let's go back to the original question about complexity. I don't think our markets have become complex at a faster rate than the rest of the world. Think about it. A newspaper person or a news agency went from being the disseminator of news by printed paper, to news delivery by TV, Internet, Twitter and Facebook. The speed of change in our industry is much like elsewhere. The key to it is customization. My example here is a current television commercial you may be familiar with. It shows people making party tapes in the 1970s and 1980s, a time-consuming and difficult task by today's standards. Now through Apple's iTunes you can download and listen to music in the sequence you want, when you want to, however you want, and wherever you are. The iPhone is complex but it allows you to really customize your music. It's not surprising that in our financial services industry we are talking about customization for people you interact with.

---

[11]At the heart of this Financial Information Exchange, or FIX Protocol, is the FIX Protocol language.

"The FIX Protocol language is comprised of a series of messaging specifications used in trade communications. Originally developed to support equities trading in the pre-trade and trade environment, it is now experiencing rapid expansion into the post-trade space, supporting straight-through processing (STP) from indications of interest (IOI) to allocations and confirmations. Additionally, it is witnessing significant growth in the fixed income, foreign exchange and listed derivative markets."

Source and expanded explanation, see http://www.fixtradingcommunity.org/pg/main/what-is-fix

Redfearn Joe, is that the ideal situation?

Mecane In a way, we are questioning the theory of markets. Much of the logic behind markets is bringing together a diverse pool of participants to let them interact. In ways, that was always the logic behind the exchanges. You had retail participants, high-frequency players, market makers, institutions and others all coming together, all interacting. You didn't know who you were trading against. The logic was to diversify the flow as much as possible. My belief today? What's being tested now is moving things in the opposite direction.

There were basically two phases in the growth of trading in ATSs,[12] internalizers,[13] and in other venues. The first phase focused on saving transaction costs on an exchange. The more recent push – and a lot of the more recent growth – is because of this whole segmentation effect. People want to interact and trade with better quality order flow. People want to trade against the retail flow. They want to trade against institutional flows if they know it is institutional on the other side, and not another high-frequency firm. It is a very rational economic logic. But it does go in the direction of "unconsolidating" the flows that historically have generally been consolidated.[14] Look, you can argue both sides. You can easily argue that putting together diverse pools of flows is better. You can also argue this much: in an environment where people are able to select who they are trading against – and are able to customize their liquidity for that type of customer – the more granular you customize the interactions among counterparties, the better is the result for everybody. Our RLP at least moved the process forward. And this goes back to Brett's point. We had almost 2 years of negotiations in our efforts to get some rudimentary capability at a minimum – to do the same things happening in upstairs venues. Where it goes from here is hard to say.

Redfearn Joe, you guys have your retail price improvement program, RPI.[15] It is somewhat similar but obviously has some nuanced differences.

---

[12] An Alternative Trading System, subject to Regulation ATS, is a non-exchange trading venue, and is, strictly speaking, an electronic platform. ATS permits buyers and sellers to execute trades in financial instruments and include ECNS, crossing networks, and dark pools. The latter has attracted much attention because in dark pools the trading of securities is not publicly displayed, a feature popular with large institutional investors because this anonymity permits them to buy and liquidate their portfolios without other market participants seeing their footprint. Their orders are kept hidden until they are executed.

[13] Internalizers are broker dealers, typically, large Wall Street investment firms, that match orders within their own firms or "internally." This practice allows them to avoid exchange fees.

[14] Referring to how trading in US equities was conducted until the advent of Alternative Trading Systems and advanced electronic trading and since the introduction of regulatory changes in market structure ended the "monopoly" of the New York Stock Exchange and NASDAQ. Flows were "consolidated" in that sense.

[15] Detailed explanation of how this Retail Price Improvement was designed here in this press release, BATS Global Markets Receives SEC Approval For Retail Price Improvement Program, November 29, 2012. See
http://cdn.batstrading.com/resources/press_releases/BATS_RPI_Approval_112912_FINAL.pdf

Ratterman A full one-third or more of the industry equity daily volume in the USA is executed off exchange.[16] In my humble opinion, that's excessive. It is potentially hampering the quality of price formation in the public markets. I came into this business thinking that the exchange is where the price comes from in stock trading. That an exchange is something special, a central marketplace that collects all the inputs for price formation and the production of a public price. A lot of the industry is feeding off of that, but is not contributing to those prices. One-third, I think, is on the edge of the high side.[17]

Up to now, exchanges have been operating on a fair access bases. Fair access is kind of a golden stamp of what we are supposed to do. And yet we were competing with firms that didn't have the same standard so they are segmenting. And the market has gravitated toward the segmented paradigm on trading. This step that the NYSE took, and the SEC paved the way for, allows exchanges an opportunity to try to bring some of that flow back onto the NYSE.[18]

It is not enough if we're going to level the playing field. I don't know for sure if we really wanted to level the playing field by bringing down the standards of the exchanges. But that, to a certain degree, is where we are headed – and so it is an experiment. The desired effect in my mind is to protect the quality of price formation that happens out in the light.

A lot of the standards in place today were developed when the markets looked very different. A great example is fair access. It is a rule that applies if a venue has reached 5% of the volume of a security on any given day, in four out of the last 6 months. Once you cross that threshold, you are compelled to behave in a fair access manner.[19] That made a lot of sense back in the late 1990s or early 2000s. But today, in a fragmented world, it is easy for ten venues to be a much larger percent of the market in aggregate. But on an individual basis, none of them have to reach 5% in order to maintain their business model. Looking at some of these thresholds it becomes a matter of bringing – and compelling – some of that price formation back into the light. That should be done in such a way that the price formation process happens on my exchange. In this manner, you would have those venues participate in the price formation process instead of staying completely dark.[20]

---

[16] "Off-exchange" is all equity trading volume executed away from exchanges in the USA via the consolidated tape and includes off-exchange trading on dark pools, wholesalers, and in upstairs trading.

[17] In a follow-up note for this chapter in 2015, BATS stated: "The BATS's stance has changed since this time as, as in detailed conversation with a broad group of customers, we've received the message that the trading community isn't uncomfortable with one-third of volume being executed off-exchange. In fact, the market sees value in off-exchange trading and we've come to realize that an exchange isn't the perfect place for every trade."

[18] BATS subsequently pressed for Alternative Trading Systems to fully disclose their rules publicly.

[19] Refers to the Reg ATS 5% threshold that forces dark pools to display quotes publicly and provide "fair access" to their markets.

[20] See follow-up footnote 3 for this chapter.

We are certainly a fan of incremental change, and then coming back later to make regulatory changes that truly fit the current market. We've got a few minor differences. At the end of the day, it is the same thing – we will provide a potentially better execution experience for retail orders on the exchange so that both parties can kind of know whom they are trading with, and step away from the full access paradigm.

I would encourage the SEC to think about ways to raise the standards a bit so that we can bring back to the light of the exchange more of the activity that is happening off the exchanges – to bolster the value of the price formation.

Redfearn So you guys don't think that all of the last sales in the broker crossing networks, automatically hitting the tape, contribute to price discovery?

Mahoney I agree, we all report to the same tape and that is where price discovery happens. You are seeing the actual reports. Ultimately there has to be some change in how rule-writing works. I run a dark pool ATS and have one rule-writing process. Then I sit with Joe on a board of our joint venture, the New York Block Exchange,[21] which is a facility of the exchange that had a different rule-writing process. Implementing a new idea takes me a year and a half in that world. But I can have an idea implemented in 30 days in this new world, in the regulatory process for ATSs. I do think there is going to be some basic fundamental reevaluation in this regard.

Mecane The question is actually around pre-trade as well as post-trade transparency. Certainly, we have the latter. We have post-trade because everything is taped, meaning trade information is public after the trade is executed. The part that isn't is the pre-transparency piece.

Redfearn Bob [Schwartz] was asking earlier today, how fast is too fast? In our trading markets today, we moved from seconds to milliseconds and now to microseconds. In some cases, trading is as fast as sub-ten micros. What is the speed of a bullet? Generally, a bullet can travel a 1000 m in a second. That means a bullet would travel 1 m in a millisecond. Which then basically means that somebody could literally trade ten times in a 200 μs turnaround market – in the same amount of time, it takes a bullet to travel 1 m. We are talking fast, really fast! We are pushing the edges with clients, as all the markets continue to move as fast as they possibly can. This is innovation, but where does the speed race end?

Ratterman At the end of the day, latency equals risk. It is that simple. In today's markets, we often hear the words front running in the wrong context. Front running is illegal. It is knowing the contents of somebody's order and trading in front of it for your own interest when, as your first priority, you theoretically are supposed to protect your client's interest. That is front running. By comparison, being able to put an order on the market before somebody else can do that, is not front running. It is minimizing the risk you have as a firm, and being willing to display your risk to the world in being immediately executable. From our role as an exchange, we think about speed as simply the mitigation of the risk that market makers and the other players are exposed to.

---

[21] NYSE Euronext filed with the SEC to cease operation of the New York Block Exchange, its joint electronic block trading venture with BIDS Trading, to take effect, February 28, 2013.

The slower you are, the more probable it is that your results will not meet your expectations when you try to act in the market. Too fast really is a matter of how much risk is being taken out of the system. We think that the speeds of the systems that are available – the networks, the switches, the servers – should be optimized so that there are no unnecessary delays between a trading decision inside of a shop and one that is active in the market. It should be the case whether you are posting a displayed order, or are trying to take liquidity that you see. It would be our job as a facilitator of those exposing and transferring risk to take as much of that risk out of the equation as possible.

Mecane The speed question goes back to my statement earlier about DMMs[22] and our market structure. We have a market structure that says that the first person at the top of the book at every protective venue gets the order. It is pretty logical that you will basically have a race to be first in line. Is that good or bad? People kind of have religion around that answer. I am not sure whether it is good or bad. I don't know if the debate about race in and of itself makes sense. Clearly, we are getting diminishing levels of improvement. But at the same time, technology advances with innovations – people are now talking about microwave related capabilities in the trading markets. How can this microwave approach improve the latency performance over fiber today? What is next after microwave? Some sort of laser technology, something along those lines? I think it will continue to evolve. Whoever is faster determines who wins and who doesn't.

Mahoney The interesting comparison would be what happens in a venue like the BIDS dark pool. Because we are focused on size. Speed is not really relevant. Our infrastructure needs are not as significant as an exchange. As you pointed out, the larger the block, the less people will care about the speed.

Redfearn George, some strategies are very short term and need co-location and high-speed direct data. Other strategies are longer term and thrive based upon longer alpha signals, certainly longer than those that rely upon 5–10 s signals.[23] The longer term strategies don't necessarily need all that high-speed infrastructure. You are saying that many in the institutional community are looking for some 10 μs market access? What is driving that? Is that necessary for institutions as well?

Kledaras They are looking to be on the same level playing field in their speed of executions as other market participants, because some of these players who are involved in high-frequency trading, for example, are sensitive to arbitrage. Technology is getting much cheaper. In fact, we're collaborating with some technology vendors to achieve this goal and to bring down speed to under a 100 ns. It is happening all over the world.

[22]These are Designated Market Makers on the floor at the New York Stock Exchange. DMMs were introduced in 2008, replacing NYSE specialists who were responsible for maintaining fair and orderly markets for assigned sets of listed companies.

[23]This is referring to algorithmic trading that professionals will be familiar with. For example, "alpha strategies" at some quantitative hedge funds, measured in several minutes, do not have a special need for ultra-low latency.

We do a lot of work with a big technology company in the USA for trading equities in Mexico. The company teamed up with Carnegie Mellon a couple of years ago, and they just rolled out a new matching engine for the trading community. Right now, this matching engine has a turnaround time of about 15 ms with plans to reduce that time even further.

Now they are starting to take a closer look at dark pools. It is fun to go into the marketplace with new offerings, because you have that classic tug of war between traders who want everything real cheap and brokers and exchanges who want to bring in order flow. So, this company and Carnegie Mellon want to keep the price of their services on the high end so they can make money.

Redfearn Kevin, if you are trying to pull counterparties together to get some large orders done – something a little chunkier than the average 200 share trade – what are your average execution sizes? And is speed relevant for you?

Callahan It is relevant but in a different way. It is clear that different market participants have different needs. For speed it is very clear. As Joe was saying, a market maker who is out on a thousand names with a quote needs to update those quotes if relevant news comes out in Europe, for example. To George's point, even institutions that are trading don't want to be the last one sitting with a stale quote. Speed is critical for that. But an institutional investor looking to buy or sell a large position in a small-cap stock has a different time perspective. For us, time is very important. We deliberately slow down the market. We have call auctions that run for 5 min, which seems like an eternity in today's high-frequency market. The idea is to bring in liquidity that is on the sidelines. That liquidity may be in a portfolio, but it is not being actively traded in the market.

Our average print size is about 50,000 shares, and the average daily volume (ADV) of the stocks we trade is about 500,000 shares. So 5 min may feel like an eternity. But if an institutional trader can buy 10% of the average daily volume in 5 min, that is actually much faster than it could expect to execute using say, algorithms or DMA. In a typical hour they wouldn't have accumulated that much liquidity in a 5 min time frame. It may seem slow, but what we are trying to do is bring in liquidity that is not actively exposed to the markets.

Redfearn Being the fastest participant, and getting in front of the trading queue, is part of the Reg NMS competitive paradigm; and ensuring automated quotes so that quotes would be accessible is another part. Critics once said that it was not always possible to access the specialists' quotes on the NYSE prior to Reg NMS changes in our market structure. Today, we have a different question regarding quote accessibility, which is the time that it takes to access a quote that might actually be even longer than the maximum duration of the posted quote. Is it a problem if quotes are being posted in the market and are then disappearing – canceled – before somebody, even the fastest traders, can hit them?

Ratterman That makes sense if a quote is on the system and disappears before anybody could even see and hit it. What value is that to the price formation process? It certainly is an activity that you would want to look at as an exchange – and we do.

The vast majority of quotations on our market don't fall into that category. But it is completely logical. A quote you can never see is not really adding to the price formation processes. You want to discourage that behavior.

There is a legitimate debate about how we can improve the overall quality. Even though nobody may see an incoming order, someone coming in to trade in that spread could bump up against an order they never saw, and thus receive price improvement. And that is not a bad thing – even though these orders may not be actionable all the time. But in this category – which is a small category – they are nonetheless executable. That's because the moment that they are on the exchange, they are executable to anybody.

Redfearn We have in many respects a one-size-fits-all market. All of our market rules generally apply to all securities, regardless of their characteristics. Tick sizes, access fees, rebates – a lot of factors apply across the board, even though some stocks are highly liquid and other stocks are not very liquid. As a result, we have, among other things, a debate about appropriate minimum tick sizes. The SEC wrote a paper about it, and the Commission is talking about having a roundtable on the issue.[24] This is a controversial topic. Is it time to launch a pilot in an attempt to widen spreads, or to change the minimum trading increment for illiquid stocks?

Mahoney Harold Bradley said it was hard to trade small-cap stocks back in the day. It has always been hard to trade them. Large-cap stocks subsidized small-cap stock trading for broker dealers and specialists. The lack of liquidity seen now in small, mid-size caps is probably appropriate. They should be harder to trade because there is a smaller market capitalization and, therefore, less volume. If you were paid a nickel to trade very liquid large-cap stocks, you could afford to subsidize the more thinly traded stocks, because you would be making money from that client on one side – and you made tighter markets all around. Now that no longer exists – all stocks trade on their own merit. It is probably the right answer.

Redfearn But today it is a challenge for somebody to display liquidity in an illiquid name with a naturally wide spread – because it is easier to jump in front of that liquidity by a penny with little risk. With a wider, possibly a nickel increment, you would potentially have the ability to aggregate more size at the quoted prices if the tick is not so tight. With this, the riskless trading, or penny jumping in front of display quotes, might be tougher, right?

Mecane I agree with Harold that trading small-cap stocks was never easy. We shouldn't fool ourselves that these types of experiments will have a dramatic impact on the current market structure. We would all agree that the market doesn't work as well in the small and mid-cap stocks as it does in the large-cap stock – in terms of

[24] See SEC Roundtable Discusses Decimalization and Tick Sizes. Jonathan Weiner, Mark Wood/Katten, Muchin, Rosenman. February 12, 2013. http://www.jdsupra.com/legalnews/sec-roundtable-discusses-decimalization-79054/

liquidity and incentivizing market participants and liquidity providers. Should we try different things that could perhaps incentivize more liquidity providers? Our view is that it is at least worth an experiment to find out.

To Brett's point: if there isn't an ability to step in front of people that do these things by only a penny increment, does it incentivize people to provide more liquidity, to display more, to perhaps be able to capture more spread? That is generally viewed by the SEC as a negative thing.

Is it worth an experiment to try and see if you can change the behavior of liquidity providers with a wider spread increment? In our opinion it is at least worth trying.

Mahoney I will say it again. I think high-frequency traders probably can play those games anyway. I don't think that the problem is small-cap, thinly traded stocks. It is that you have a computer trading 100–200 shares in front of people. It is hard to trade in this environment. We should try to fix it and be realistic. But there is very little that we can do to make this market as liquid as the market for large-cap stocks.

Callahan We already have a nickel market, a dime market, and a quarter market. We had an auction yesterday in a company called Collectors Universe (NASDAQ: CLCT). It is a 100 million dollar market-cap company on NASDAQ, and it trades 18,000 shares a day. The quote was 13.63 bid and 13.75 offer. It now has a 12 cent spread. If you look across the ADVs you would find a direct inverse correlation between trading volume and spreads. The lower the trading volume, the higher the spread. So the market already allows for spreads to widen where liquidity is scarce. Mandating that these stocks only trade in nickels – rather than letting the free market decide – takes the market back 20 years to when the market traded in quarters, eighths, and sixteenths.

We have a competitive market today. People can quote in pennies, nickels or dimes, or even quarters depending on the stock. As it turns out, more thinly traded stocks have a wider spread because there is risk in taking the other side of a trade. I just don't see what the pilot would accomplish. As for this idea that we will bring back old-fashioned market making and research coverage to small and micro-cap companies? I don't think that nickels will accomplish this.

Redfearn If the trading increment was wider, would someone then feel a bit more comfortable displaying liquidity at their price? Wouldn't it be harder for somebody else to jump in front of their quote if they had to do so by a full nickel?

Mahoney Nobody ever displayed liquidity. I just don't remember that time (laughter).

But let's talk about the New York Stock Exchange. Once upon a time, the best brokers would keep your order inside their paper notebook, and they would keep it all very quiet. If you showed your order to anybody then everybody knew it! It is the same problem you have today.

Ratterman In any event, now I think there will be a pilot. I was with the SEC several times, most recently 2 weeks ago. The SEC, as a result of The Jobs Act,[25] is likely to do something. I also believe it is completely foolish to think that if you widen the spreads then market makers will be happy to take in all the extra money – and that somebody will magically initiate research on a stock and that, because of the research, more retail clientele will start trading the stock. That is just a completely imaginary outcome.

There is some value in widening the available spread. Today's market making is predominantly by automated market makers on a stock by stock basis. If a stock makes money, they will make markets; if it doesn't, they will turn the dials down. In that kind of world, market makers may put up a little bit more size in these securities if there is a wider spread and more opportunity for dollars. There is some possibility that the size available and the reference market will be more stable in a tick-constrained world. That is worth more than a pilot – and there will be a pilot.

Redfearn Let's open this panel to the audience.

Justin Schack [Rosenblatt Securities Inc.] If you accept Joe Ratterman's premise – which I think is spot on – that latency equals risk, then it strikes me that the fundamental public policy question about speed is this: Does the end investor have access to good enough speed? Does the end investor have enough speed in a commercially available way, so that it is not substantially at a disadvantage in the marketplace?

Kledaras Prices for access to products that reduce the turnaround time – latency – have been driven down over the last few months. We are talking now about major savings in the hundreds of thousands of dollars for the industry. It is a pretty dramatic price change. And further improvements in latency and in speed are coming, with new and better technology.

Redfearn Most brokers, certainly the large brokers, have had to invest in co-location, and direct data feeds – and have had to implement anti-gaming and a whole slew of other technologies to make sure that institutional client orders are trading at a competitive level with the fastest opportunist market participants. But it is true that as we continue to push the limits, there is always a question about some gap – and whether or not the gap with the fastest players creates an opportunistic zone for some.[26]

---

[25] The Jumpstart Our Business Startups Act (JOBS Act) became law on April 5 2012. The Jobs Act was enacted in the US to provide private companies more access to capital, and to make it easier for more companies to become public on US exchanges.

[26] The moderator did not specify or identify players who might be availing of this opportunity from this "gap." However, it is well known that some of the high-speed trading firms invested in technology can trade "faster" than some of the trading firms at the big banks. "These guys are going to continue to push the limit of faster and faster technology and optimizing their systems and shave off a microsecond here and a microsecond there," one trading professional explained. In a follow-up, Redfearn noted: "There is always going to be some technology speed gap and, depending on the size of that gap and how it works, there is an opening created for opportunistic market participants, which ultimately is part of the competitive landscape we grapple with."

Kledaras For example, 68% of the revenue at one technology vendor we know is accounted for by its co-location services.[27]

Mahoney Are you trading or are you investing? If your time frame is long enough, speed is almost irrelevant. Whether you are an institutional investor or retail investor, I still think that this is a great market structure for retail investors. If you can trade from your house, where ever it is (say in the Midwest), you can buy 200 shares of stock, pay only five dollars commission, and be able to sell that stock in a year from now. A year from now that stock will have moved based on company fundamentals, not on what a market maker quoted. But you bought that stock for only five dollars in commissions, because they were routing the order flow to some retail provider which allowed them to pass the savings of execution costs back to their clients. I still think that is advantageous. I agree with Brett that institutional investing and these algorithms on the institutional side are a really sophisticated phenomena.

Redfearn Looking back three or so years ago, there were times where those opportunity zones, for lack of a better term, were pretty wide.

Anthony Fortunato [Instinet] Do you think it is possible – without eliminating dark pool participation – to narrow the spreads in the dark pools?

Mahoney Is it a minimum trade increment, or is it a quote increment? Right now you can only quote in pennies. It's not clear how this will turn out. Will it be that you can only trade at .05? That means that the institutional investors have to pay the full spread to trade, which means they only trade once every 7 years! If you talk to people now, they don't even want to cross the penny spread, much less a five cent spread.[28]

Bradley What is the benefit of going to a wider quote if you don't go to a wider minimum increment?

Mecane That will end up being the middle ground. Maybe it is not just about bid or offer and mid-point. Maybe you shouldn't have six decimal points with trading increments in between the penny like we do now.

---

[27] Klederas did not identify the company. However, it is noted that co-location services are a major portion of exchange revenues. For example, overall revenue from these "Access Service" fees as they are known at NASDAQ, more than doubled from $112 million in fiscal year 2008 to $239 million in fiscal year 2012, according to analyst Richard Repetto at Sandler O'Neill.

[28] Mahoney is referring to a proposed pilot program for trading small-cap stocks in wider minimum increments. The pilot eventually was approved by the Securities and Exchange Commission. See SEC Approves Pilot Program to Assess Tick Size Impact for Smaller Companies. Center for Financial Stability, May 7, 2015. http://centerforfinancialstability.org/wp/?p=5987

In a follow-up for this chapter, Mahoney said he was pondering on this panel a pilot that requires a five cent spread. The pilot program as announced appeared to allow trades to occur at the midpoint, he said. This was unclear at the time of the conference. If, however, you could only buy the stock at say, 21.00 or 21.05 – and not at the midpoint – then if you wanted to later sell the stock, it meant you had to stay at the offer, 21.05, until someone crossed the spread. "Someone has to lose! They have to sell on the bid or buy on the offer! There is no compromise, no splitting the difference. So I was being facetious, implying that no one would ever trade – and that people would sit on the bid and offer," according to Mahoney.

Redfearn Any more questions from the audience?

Neal Wolkoff I want to touch on the impact that dark liquidity has on the lit markets, and on how you can tell if and when the lit markets are actually being hurt by the dark liquidity. It seems to me that if the lit markets weren't delivering really efficient and effective price discovery, we would know about it. One of the ways you would tell if the lit markets were no longer effective anymore is, if you saw a decrease of business in the dark pools. What data and information do you guys use to determine if and when, for large names anyway, your liquidity or your price discovery function is being hurt by activity in the dark pools?

Mecane I actually disagree with the premise. I would argue in a way that there is a perverse incentive. The wider the spreads are in the lit markets, the more incentive there is for people to trade away from the lit markets because the spreads are wider. To answer your direct question, Neal, there have been academic studies on this topic. The more off-exchange trading that you have, the wider the spread tends to be, all things being equal. There is that perverse feedback.

On another matter, there is something like 1500 stock issues that have off-exchange trading percentages in excess of 50%. The overall number, as Joe said, is around one third. But you've got 1300 or so names, especially a lot of the mid- to small-cap names, that do have the vast majority of their trading off an exchange. To Tim's point, I don't think the pilot is meant to imply that we will be able to widen the spreads, and that we will then see an additional tens of thousands of shares in trading activity. But there is so much that doesn't reside on the public markets now.

Redfearn There are academic papers that argue on both sides of this issue. That said, you can calculate the off-exchange volume in active stocks like Citigroup before its reverse split, or in Bank of America today, and you will realize that quite a bit of the total off-exchange volume is from very liquid stocks, with deep order books, and price discovery that is fully intact.

Let's turn to rebates. Market makers make markets – and make money. If you look at the 30 mil ($0.003/share) access fee cap that was put in place with Reg NMS, and the related 29 mil ($0.0029/share) rebates that exchanges often pay for posted limit orders, there seems to be a built in incentive to post displayed orders.[29] This incentivizes participation in some names but perhaps does not entice the same kind of participation in the smaller, illiquid stocks. By the way, one could argue a reason for internalization in many active stocks is to avoid some of the high fees – take rates – that basically subsidize rebates paid to HFT market makers. Is our maker-taker rebate structure right, or should this be tweaked in some way that better accommodates the different characteristics among stocks to help better distribute liquidity?[30]

[29] This fee cap model was enshrined in Reg NMS, so in that sense its application is industry wide.

[30] In the maker-taker model of US exchanges, brokerages earn rebates by sending in resting orders to generate liquidity, but these brokers must pay fees if they "take" away liquidity via orders that can be executed immediately.

Mahoney Before we focus on the exchanges, I do think the lowering of the institutional commissions is a major factor in today's conflicts. There is an unintended consequence when you go from six cents to half a penny – because the take rate on exchanges becomes a dramatically larger percentage of the fees that a client pays. This discussion is related to the fact that the explicit commissions that institutions once made are reduced dramatically. And so that influenced a lot of behavior. Brokers started to internalize – because if you are getting five cents commissions you could afford a small fee to the exchange. But if you are only making 30 mils commissions, and paying 28 of it to the exchange, it was a very different economic reality. It is a lot. If you are thinking about rates, it's not just the exchanges and the maker-taker model. It is the fabric of the entire marketplace.[31]

Mecane I agree. A lot of behavior over the last 5–10 years is trying to force things in this way. Maker taker clearly drives the takers crazy. At the same time, it is one of the primary tools that ends up being used to incentivize liquidity providers. The rebate is basically used to equalize the incentives of liquidity providers, a lot of whom are providing liquidity in the ATSs and the dark pools; a lot of whom are displaying on the public markets. That rebate basically equalizes it. Certainly people can have religion about whether the rebate should be banished, or the take rates should be lower. All that is fine. But you can't address that in isolation, you have to address that in the context of broader market structure.

Redfearn This was a superb panel. Thank you.

[31] The standard institutional commission in the US was between 5 and 7 cents in the 1980s and 1990s. As Mahoney explained in a follow-up: "Now you get paid 50 mills or 0.5 of a penny – around 10% of the old rate. As there is less money does everyone need to change their behavior? It was easy to pay an exchange fee that was 10% of you total commission, now you need to pay 60%."

Chapter 7
The Need for Further Change

Nina Mehta, Stephen Bookbinder, Chris Concannon, Cheryl Knopp, William O'Brien, and Neal Wolkoff

Nina Mehta We can safely assume market structure is a moving target, constantly in a state of flux. Some would agree that US market structure is the eighth wonder of the world. And yet others might think it is simply a broken toy of the regulators or, indeed, of the financial services industry at large. In this light, let me start by asking the panel for their top one or two regulatory wishes, or thoughts about change.

Stephen Bookbinder The crowdfunding plan and the Jobs Act[1], in my opinion, are a good place to start in terms of wishes. Market structure is about the public markets. I will, however, confine my comments specifically to the private markets. Their evolution, and the regulations associated with the private markets, is actually moving in the right direction.

---

[1] The Security and Exchange Commission's (SEC) crowdfunding plan is a requirement in the 2012 Jumpstart Our Business Startups (JOBS) Act, a 2012 law to spur job growth and, at the time of writing, to permit small business owners to raise as much as $1 million through unaccredited investors

N. Mehta (✉)
Bloomberg News, New York City, UK

S. Bookbinder
GreenCrest Capital, New York City, UK

C. Concannon
Virtu Financial, New York, NY, USA

C. Knopp
Liquidnet, New York, NY, USA

W. O'Brien
Direct Edge, Jersey City, NJ, USA

N. Wolkoff
American Stock Exchange, New York, NY, USA

R.A. Schwartz et al. (eds.), *Rapidly Changing Securities Markets*,
Zicklin School of Business Financial Markets Series,
DOI 10.1007/978-3-319-54588-2_7

Cheryl Knopp At Liquidnet, we always look at regulatory change through the eyes of our institutional clients who represent and manage the money of individual investors. But in terms of regulatory change, it really needs to be a wholesale approach, looking out to restore the individual investor's confidence so that they will put their money back into the market – whether or not that involves the Securities and Exchange Commission bringing in, for example, Tradeworx,[2] or learning more about high-frequency trading to help achieve this goal.

Chris Concannon[3] I have seen numerous regulatory changes. Some led to unintended consequences. I am not really looking for massive regulatory change. Let me ask: Is anyone aware of the recent accusations of rampant front running in the markets? To this date I haven't seen any evidence nor a case brought as a result.

We continue to point out that the industry is layered with fraudulent behavior. People write and sell books on the topic. I do believe in an upgrade of our US surveillance system. I agree with gaining the confidence of investors through premium surveillance in US equities. We certainly have this premium market, yet our surveillance is second rate compared to some of the surveillances in options markets or elsewhere. We are having a liquidity crisis that is reflected in the reduced share volumes today. The real issue is the liquidity in our books, and in the less liquid names. The chatter from the buy-side is about their challenges in trying to trade stocks they once traded more easily.[4]

William O'Brien This topic reminds me of running Direct Edge,[5] one of the largest stock exchanges in the world. You don't change one or two things; you need a broader vision than that. What are you trying to achieve? What is your overall mission? Some 15 years ago, the SEC explicitly said its mission is to promote competition with a view to driving down investor explicit transaction costs as low as we possibly can.[6] It has been successful. A lot of the problems in the late 1990s and the

[2] Referring to an SEC program designed by Tradeworx of Red Bank, NJ, to help monitor and track suspicious trading activity. See To Regulate Rapid Traders, SEC Turns to One of Them, Nathaniel Popper, Ben Protess, *New York Times*, October 7, 2012. http://www.nytimes.com/2012/10/08/business/sec-regulators-turn-to-high-speed-trading-firm.html

[3] Since the conference, Chris Concannon left Virtu Financial. He was named president of BATS Global Markets in December 2014, assuming the additional role of CEO of the company in February 2015.

[4] Referring to the lack of liquidity in certain stocks including smaller names that do not have the same level of market maker support in the kind of highly automated, high-speed, and fragmented markets the speaker indirectly describes.

[5] In August 2013, Direct Edge Holdings, operator of Direct Edge, and BATS Global Markets announced their plans to merge under the BATS moniker in an all-stock transaction. The deal closed in early 2014. The owners of the new, merged entity included Goldman Sachs, Morgan Stanley, Credit Suisse and Citadel, Citigroup, and KCG Holdings.

[6] With regulatory changes and the advances in electronic trading, institutional stock trading commissions continued to shrink in the years prior to this conference. In fact, 2012 saw broker fees for US

early part of this century have disappeared.[7] Now we have new challenges. How do you deal with them in a way that preserves the benefits but also addresses today's undeniable investor confidence issues? One is to make sure you do not introduce more incremental risk into the system. The nature of risk has really changed. There is a big component of technology-related risk today, like there is in every industry. And people are waking up to that.

I always am amused when you have a stream of thought telegraphing how markets are too complicated, change is coming too fast. You hear talk about order types[8] – and how we need various fixes such as limit up, limit down[9]; a pilot program of different price increments for different-sized stocks[10]; and a minimum resting order life of half a second.[11] Those arguments really are not consistent with one another.

Forget about the technology. Focus on the conduct that has been prohibited for a long, long time. Put the regulatory cops on the beat to detect that and to improve market intelligence. Then we need to brag a little bit about that. There is an overwhelming majority of honest people in the industry. Regulators are trying to do the right thing. And I don't think they are getting as much credit as they deserve.

Neal Wolkoff I agree with Bill and Chris, surveillance and enforcement are really important aspects of investor confidence. To some extent my experience over the last few years has been in the futures market. Actually, I was trying to start a

---

stock trading decline to their lowest levels since 2006, driven in part by outflows from stock funds but also because of electronic trading coupled with the contraction in trading commissions, generally.

In 2006, the average rate for trading a New York Stock Exchange-listed share declined to 3.9 cents a share from 4.2 cents last year, according to Greenwich Associates. The average for a Nasdaq Stock Market trade dropped to 3.8 cents from 4 cents. See Broker Fees for US stock trading fell to lowest since 2006. http://www.bloomberg.com/news/articles/2012-05-31/broker-fees-for-u-s-stock-trading-fell-to-lowest-since-2006

[7] For example, there was the reported Nasdaq price-fixing scandal of the late 1990s, a scandal which resulted in a class-action lawsuit and a $910 million settlement by 30 securities firms.

[8] Basic order types include market, limit, and stop. Trading platforms today permit traders to use a multitude of other order types.

[9] Notably, Nasdaq's proposed "limit up-limit down" rule in 2011, coming in response to concerns on market volatility, was intended to prevent trades in National Market System securities from happening outside of specific price bands.

[10] See SEC asks exchanges, FINRA to submit "tick size" pilot plan, *Reuters*, Supriya Kurane, June 25, 2014, http://www.reuters.com/article/2014/06/25/sec-pilotprogram-trading-idUSL4N0P61HV20140625

[11] This is the minimum period of time an order must "rest" on an exchange to remain "valid" as in the case of a proposal, for example, by the European parliament in 2012, which sought to introduce a minimum resting time of at least 500 milliseconds for orders to remain valid on an exchange. This resting period was in response to the rapid fire and controversial aspects of high-frequency trading.

competitive futures exchange, ELX Markets.[12] But in my experience, it was close to impossible. For that matter, it would be close to impossible for anyone else. The reality is that, except in the energy asset class for crude oil, natural gas, and so on, where there are two major competing markets – the New York Mercantile Exchange, or NYMEX, and the Intercontinental Exchange, or ICE – everything else out there is, in effect, one market, at least domestically.

That said, there is this constant drum beat and crisis of investor confidence – and maybe there will always be. But there is also a danger of drawing a correlation between events we have seen – whether it is the Facebook IPO,[13] the BATS IPO,[14] even the Flash Crash,[15] and the Kraft pricing issues[16] – and then blaming that for this crisis of confidence.

Certainly these are not helping investor confidence. But we can also look at larger issues on a more macro level: For example, the aging of the US population. More baby boomers are preparing for retirement. We had a market collapse at the time of the financial crisis in 2008, following on the heels of the dot-com market collapse of 2000. Who knows what exactly is damaging investor confidence?

Many are focused on the BATS's IPO, for example, as a reason for not wanting to participate in the equity markets – as opposed to another possibility for this diminution in investor confidence: More people will be retiring in five years. Think about it: I have seen a higher amount of risk in my 401(k) without having a defined benefit plan to back that up.[17] I have to be really careful about risk. Things are never that simple and black and white.

---

[12] ELX Markets, formerly ELX Futures, launched in 2009, was no longer active as of writing in 2015. Wolkoff was a former CEO at this electronic futures exchange with its headquarters in New York City.

[13] See Facebook IPO: What the %$#! happened? Julianne Pepitone, *CNNMoney*, May 23, 2012, http://money.cnn.com/2012/05/23/technology/facebook-ipo-what-went-wrong/index.htm

[14] The BATS IPO was scrapped after a software glitch sent its shares plunging to a fraction of a cent within seconds of the attempted IPO on March 23, 2012.

[15] The Flash Crash of May 6, 2010, lasted about 36 min, erasing 998.5 points or about 9% in the Dow Jones Industrial Average, and then quickly recouping the losses as the various indexes rapidly rebounded in this high-speed, electronic trading phenomenon. At the time, it was a record one-day point decline on an intraday basis in the history of Dow Jones Industrial Average.

[16] Price of the stock (Nasdaq: KRFT) surged 25% within 1 min soon after the market opened. The glitch was blamed on a broker error by Nasdaq that affected multiple exchanges. "Investors were hit with another stock-trading glitch Wednesday, this one in a household name – Kraft Foods – which saw dozens of trades canceled when a broker error caused shares to soar shortly after the opening bell," according to *The Wall Street Journal*. See *WSJ* story, Kraft Hit by Trading Glitch, October 3, 2012, Alexandra Scaggs and Matt Jarzemsky.

[17] Referring to the "risk" differences between a "defined contribution plan," or a 401(k), as it is commonly called vs. the traditional defined benefits which, in effect, "guarantee" participants pension payouts in retirement, regardless of market conditions. The former 401(k)s have hugely overtaken the latter plans in terms of participants in recent years.

There are obvious things that should be enforced because of certain activity out there such as spoofing.[18] But that is not really about a wholesale change of rules and regulations. The fact that the securities markets today have a level of competition, and an ease of access and exit to the market, is great. I like the impact of the Jobs Act; I like its focus on small-cap companies, facilitating public access to capital markets. I would welcome pilot programs in tick sizes.[19] I like the focus on reenergizing the IPO market.[20]

Mehta What are your thoughts about SEC Commissioner Daniel Gallagher's speech the other day? He said the SEC should conduct a broad review of regulatory and market structure.[21] For example, he asked whether self-regulation had passed its prime. Should there be self-regulatory organizations (SROs), and should exchanges be SROs? Should they have a limitation on liability for the problems that they cause? What about the market data aspects of SROs? Let me also ask, should exchanges remain as SROs? And if they were no longer SROs what would happen? Could I buy a stock through the NYSE brokerage firm on the corner? Could they become a broker and could I become their client?

Concannon These are no longer the same stock exchanges. There once was a member-controlled, floor-based system the industry decided to demutualize and convert to something else.[22] Nevertheless, they are still self-regulatory organizations. They have to file rules and enforce those rules on their members. I was intrigued by Commissioner Gallagher's speech. We have challenges in how many exchanges we will have. We have new licenses coming online. There are ten or more US stock exchanges today.[23] Is 25 the right number? I don't know. But right now the statute says, in effect, we could have many more. The SEC needs to look at that.

O'Brien Commissioner Gallagher's speech was bold. I have a lot of respect for him because he suggests an approach along the lines in my opening remarks. Let's have a top-down review, as we try to establish a vision of the principles we look to advance, cutting across the regulation of all market participants – exchanges being one of them.

[18] Spoofing is the controversial trading practice of placing orders and then quickly canceling them, creating an "illusion" of up or down market movements.

[19] See footnote 7.

[20] For more, see The JOBS ACT: A New IPO Playing Field for Emerging Growth Companies. Goodwin Procter April 25, 2012. http://www.goodwinprocter.com/Publications/Newsletters/Client-Alert/2012/0425_JOBS-ACT-A-New-IPO-Playing-Field-For-Emerging-Growth-

[21] See Market 2012: Time for a Fresh Look at Equity Market Structure and Self-Regulation Commissioner Daniel M. Gallagher, SIFMA's 15th Annual Market Structure Conference, Oct. 4, 2012 http://www.sec.gov/News/Speech/Detail/Speech/1365171491376

[22] Demutualization is the conversion of an exchange from mutual status – a member-owned exchange – to ownership by a private or public company. The New York Stock Exchange demutualizated in 2006 when it becomes a for-profit, publicly traded company. And as noted by one analyst, this gives the exchanges an incentive to start managing for profit and the brokers an incentive to become more competitive.

[23] As of August 2015, there were 11 US stock exchanges, according to a Reuters report.

Let me add this: Much credit is deserved by Professor Robert Schwartz here at Baruch College. What was the title, Bob, of your conference here last year? It was "The Economic Function of a Stock Exchange." You were asking that question a year ago. More questions than answers usually come out of these conferences.

One answer? Exchanges have to foster a reliable network. Do I get the same type of outcome every time? Do I get a predictable outcome every time? That comes from having rules of the road, and having everybody understand them. This goes back to my other comment, am I protected from the bad guys? You have to work really hard to say that the bad guys aren't people who get a better outcome than you. But there is conduct that has to be prescribed, and people have to detect it, punish it, and hopefully deter it. There is a role that exchanges still play along these lines, whether they are self-regulatory organizations or not.

Wolkoff The exchanges still perform some important SRO functions. I don't think it is valuable to take away from them, say the oversight of listings and the oversight of the IPO market, or the first day of trading in a new stock and how that is organized. Although the SRO function for most exchanges is subcontracted to FINRA,[24] it doesn't mean that the responsibility for surveillance and enforcement completely goes away for each exchange. That issue becomes most significant now in terms of real-time market management. Some of that is probably addressed with automation and circuit breakers when stocks hit defined trading parameters, especially during periods of pronounced volatility, and trading is halted. But who takes the lead when something happens in real time? Can any one exchange be entrusted with making a decision on behalf of the other exchanges at important moments, and at times of crisis? In my view, there is sometimes weakness and inconsistency in this decision-making process.

Mehta IPOs are part of a regulatory function that exchanges provide. That obviously was an issue this year with BATS and at Nasdaq with the Facebook IPO.[25] Because Nasdaq's largest customers have written to the SEC saying that the regulatory interest of Nasdaq – which is to have an orderly market – hits right up against that commercial interest with the decision that they made.[26]

Wolkoff You can't say you have immunity for taking regulatory actions that work out well. By the same token, you don't have immunity if a regulatory action turns out to have been a bad decision. That said, BATs has not received the credit it deserves. Everybody has acknowledged problems of their own. There are very few

[24] The Financial Industry Regulatory Authority.

[25] See footnote 11.

[26] For instance, in a letter to the Securities and Exchange Commission dated August 2012, Citigroup claimed that decisions made by Nasdaq, the second-largest US equity trading venue, in the IPO were aimed at protecting profits rather than member firms. "Market participants suffered hundreds of millions of dollars of losses as a result of Nasdaq's profit-driven conduct prior to and during the Facebook IPO, not as a result of protected regulatory activity by Nasdaq, or routine system failures," Citigroup wrote. "Nasdaq should not be permitted to hide behind regulatory immunity."

markets that can say, "I have never had a technology issue." BATs had a technology issue in the most embarrassing public way possible. When it couldn't remedy the problem it simply put its IPO off, and to this day has not had an IPO.[27] Do I think Nasdaq made the best decisions that it could have made under the circumstances? No, I don't. Do I still think they were fulfilling some sort of regulatory obligation in getting the IPO priced and into the market? Yes, I do. It is a hard line.

I was at the NYMEX many years ago in charge of compliance. We were once sued for a compliance action. We had to take it through the courts, and, it is one of the seminal cases in immunity.[28] Every time you act you are worried about somebody coming back and saying, you could have made a better decision. The answer is always going to be yes, I probably could have made a better decision given everything you do after the fact.

Mehta There is a lot of talk about leveling the playing field, to borrow the language the NYSE and Nasdaq have used to describe the roles and responsibilities of exchanges and brokers – and what they are permitted in terms of the regulatory filing process, flexibility of changing rules on the fly, and so on. Let's talk about if there was a movement toward making that more even, and about permitting exchanges more latitude to do some of the things brokers are allowed to do. Chris and Cheryl, if there was a more comparable treatment of exchanges and brokers, would you guys be comfortable going through the process?

Knopp As a general position, Liquidnet is very transparent. It has a transparent relationship with its regulators. We deal with regulators all over the globe. We support transparency, so I think it is something that we wouldn't have a problem with.

Concannon We have to look at the automation review policy enforced since the 1990s.[29] The exchanges comply with it even though it is voluntary. All of the exchanges take it very seriously, and the SEC examiners who conduct an inspection

---

[27] As of writing in 2015, there were reports about BATS aiming to make another effort at an IPO of BATS as early as 2016, or the coming months, under new president and chief executive Chris Concannon.

[28] See Edward MANDELBAUM and Cooperative Trading Services, Incorporated, Plaintiffs, v.NEW YORK MERCANTILE EXCHANGE, R. Patrick Thompson, Ronald G. Oppenheimer, James Morrissey, Stuart Smith, and Does 1 Through 10 Inclusive, Defendants.

No. 93 Civ. 8302 (AGS). August 1, 1995. United States District Court, S.D. New York.

[29] As background, the Securities and Exchange Commission published a policy statement on the automated systems of SROs Automated Systems of Self-Regulatory Organizations (II). Stating in part: "On November 16, 1989, the Securities and Exchange Commission ("SEC" or "Commission") published its first Automation Review Policy ("ARP I")[1] in which it stated its view that the self-regulatory organizations ("SROs"), on a voluntary basis, should establish comprehensive planning and assessment programs to determine systems capacity and vulnerability". At that time, the Commission noted the impact that systems problems and failures could have on public investors, broker-dealer risk exposure, and market efficiency and, as a result, urged that the SROs take appropriate measures to ensure that, initially, their automated trading systems "have the capacity to accommodate current and reasonably anticipated future trading volume levels adequately and to respond to localized emergency conditions" (ARP I at 12). See http://www.sec.gov/divisions/marketreg/arp-ii.htm

expect them to comply. Still, the conversion from voluntary to a forced rule doesn't change the exchange behavior. You have to take a step back and ask whether the automation review is all that successful. Yet we are talking about doing more with it because of incidents that happen. Technology breaks, there are software bugs, things happen in a complex world. The automation review policy may or may not help. But it has already been in effect all these years.

Mehta Steve and Cheryl, why do companies today not go public as frequently as in the past? Talk in the media and chatter is that companies shy away from public markets. In part, this is because of the problems that have occurred, including the Flash Crash and technology problems.

Bookbinder There is a bigger decision that companies make in not going public. It does not necessarily have to do with technology. I see a lot of companies delaying their public offerings as long as they can. Your company, Bloomberg, is a perfect example. It will never go public. Why do companies go public? Because they need capital. If you could raise capital on the private markets there really is not a reason to go public.

The evolution of that marketplace is such that there is a lot of money out there when people want to invest in private companies. We are seeing that day after day. If a private company is successful, it has good management through venture capital companies, private investors, and family offices. There are lots of people willing to invest in private companies. We are seeing an influx of investors in private companies. Technology has nothing to do with it. It is the need for capital, the ability to gain capital, and the private market is there. That is why companies stay private longer.

Mehta Do you think the Jobs Act will encourage more companies to go public, or will it help companies before they go public in terms of getting investors?

Bookbinder For the most part, the Jobs Act is a bit of a farce. I don't see the Jobs Act really affecting the balance between companies going public and being private. Arthur Levitt, the former Chairman of the SEC,[30] also mentioned that he didn't think it was necessarily a good thing for the marketplace. It is not going to create a lot of jobs. It does allow companies to stay private longer. It makes the ability to list as a public company easier if you are under a certain size.

But, for the most part, the Jobs Act is really for small companies. It is really for the mom and pop organizations. If you want to start a cleaning company, or a construction company, for example. With a limited number of employees, it allows you through crowdfunding, to raise capital, and from that standpoint it is good. But if you are a technology company, or if you are a large organization with hundreds of employees and you are successful, the Jobs Act won't affect you. And it won't affect your decision to go public, or to stay private. Again, it all goes back to capital.

On the flip side, the evolution of the marketplace is such that investors, whether municipalities, pension funds, or family offices, are now looking at private companies for investment opportunity. When Facebook went public, there were lots of different

[30] Arthur Levitt served as SEC Chairman from 1993 to 2001.

reasons why it failed. But, if you had invested three, four, five dollars a share, you are still doing pretty well. It is those people who invested toward the end of its private life cycle who lost a lot of money. Investors are looking at private companies as opportunities. I don't think technology or regulation really will affect that.

Knopp Back to the initial question about why companies are staying private longer. There are several reasons, as Steve outlined. A lot of these companies want to focus on running and building their business. Once you become a public company, you are answering to analysts and to the market. A lot of these companies would stay private forever if they were able to get the capital they want.

Steve mentioned institutions looking to this marketplace. About 66% of our membership at Liquidnet wants alternative investments as part of their growth priorities. In the private shares team I am running, I am essentially bringing to these companies more money than has ever been focused on them before.[31] The Liquidnet membership – that is, our institutional customers – account for $12 trillion in equity assets under management. Even if it is a small slice, it is bringing this money to private companies to enable them to stay private longer.[32]

Institutional investment is filling the gap, by also providing secondary liquidity to the venture capital funds that want to sell their private company holdings in order to return money to their investors. It is giving institutions the opportunity to get into positions they had been locked out of for a long time. The Jobs Act will help in that the number of shareholders a company can have before it is required to go public went from 500 shareholders to a much larger number (excluding employees).[33]

As Steve noted, these institutional investments, before a company goes public, allow the company to raise funds it needs before going out to the public markets, and it also provides some secondary liquidity for employees or early founders. That means that everybody can get back to focusing on growing their companies rather than focusing on having to do an IPO to raise capital.

Mehta How much longer are companies staying private now than a decade ago?

Knopp I would say they used to go public after five or six years. Now it's more like nine or ten years. In any event, we see all this – that is, raising a private round from an institution – as a step along the way to an IPO. It is not necessarily that these

[31] Before institutions started investing more heavily in private companies, the well-known funding option for private companies was capital raising via venture capital (VC) investors. By one estimate, even if institutions earmarked 1% of their assets under management to pre-IPO investments, this would equal up to $40 billion (as of Q3 2013), which is much more than the available VC funding.

[32] The amount of capital that institutions are investing in private companies is a very small portion of their assets under management. However, these investments are providing capital to private companies that would otherwise have to go public in order to raise funds to operate. By tapping these institutions, the companies can delay going public while still raising the capital they need.

[33] As of its signing into law on April 2012, the JOBS Act raised the number of shareholders a company is allowed to have before it is required to register with the Securities and Exchange Commission to 2000 total shareholders, or 500 shareholders who are not accredited investors. Certain types of shareholders are excluded from these totals.

companies will not go public. But most of our institutions are long only.[34] They will hold after the IPO. As I said, it is filling this gap; the venture capital funds need to return the money to their investors.

Mehta We have question from the floor.

Harold Bradley [Former Chief Investment Officer, the Ewing Marion Kauffman Foundation] Institutional investors in the late 1990s were effectively managed by Wall Street's big investment banks in the frothy IPO markets. Companies floated very small issuance. And institutions received allocations based on their recent history of commissions paid to the bank, and the order size for the IPO, along with promises to participate in buying more in the so-called aftermarket – meaning they would promise to buy more and not "flip" shares during sometimes crazy first day prices. A trader might indicate a willingness to buy 100,000 shares, hoping to win an allocation of 10,000 or 20,000 shares. That is what happened in a hot deal. In more recent years, hedge funds took the place of traditional institutional buyers and would often pay very high cents per share commissions in front of a "hot" IPO.

As hedge funds squeezed our traditional buy-side firms – think Morgan Stanley Asset Management, Fidelity, or T Rowe Price – the traditional firms instead took more risk and acquired private equity positions in the "hot" companies prior to the IPO. The Facebook IPO brought a lot of this activity into clearer focus. They turned to the SecondMarket[35] to buy unregistered private shares. Retail investors were clueless to this change and so were stunned when brokers called them offering unspoken-for shares in the Facebook IPO. Retail buyers acted like the institutions of the late 1990s and gave retail brokers indications for Facebook shares that exceeded what they thought would happen. Retail investors, looking for a quick profitable flip, and choking on the supply, were ultimately disappointed – Facebook traded down on the first day from the IPO price. Seems like ancient history now, for sure. That ended up being the big problem for Nasdaq and the broker dealers. I am wondering how the whole ecosystem has seemed to change. I am also wondering what implications the regulations should be looking at in regard to that.

Bookbinder I am going to correct you but I don't mean to do that.

Bradley Correct me.

Bookbinder Morgan Stanley, T Rowe Price, JP Morgan, whoever owned stock pre-IPO were not able to sell that stock until six months after the IPO. It wasn't their orders going into the marketplace. They had to sit on the sidelines.

---

[34] Long only is a feature or policy of many mutual funds, and it refers to a policy of only holding "long" positions in assets and securities.

[35] Founded in 2004, New York City-based SecondMarket (formerly Restricted Stock Partners) offers an electronic facility and a service for private companies and investment funds seeking to do tender offers or share buybacks. The company also has a trading unit for illiquid assets, including private company stock. See company website: www.SecondMarket.com

Bradley I agree with you. But it was the naïve retail customers back then who were left to purchase shares traditionally gobbled up by mutual funds and other big players.

Bookbinder That is right and that is part of the issue. And as for the institutional players that wanted to get in there – and I also need to correct you – most of those institutions bought directly through Facebook. SecondMarket is more of a retail platform. Cheryl and I represent institutional platforms, by the way.

O'Brien There is a fascinating tension here. We spend a lot of time on the conference circuit talking about two-tier markets, and people having certain capabilities that others don't have. There is also this push for creating secondary markets that have much less regulation, and a much more constricted user base. It is just kind of hard for me to square that circle.

Knopp I wouldn't consider it – the market for pre-IPO investments by institutions – unregulated. But back to the question about the retail piece of the Facebook transaction. Here is what we are trying to do at Liquidnet – and are actually doing with private companies – in bringing these opportunities to our institutions: We are working with the companies to provide a solution, rather than bringing together a hundred high-level rich individuals who are in it for the bump at the IPO. Bringing them a long-only investment from an institution, and one who will hold after the IPO. This was part of the challenge. Facebook did nothing to control its caps table before its IPO. They get to look at an investor base that is very different from what Facebook built their investor base upon right before its IPO.[36]

Mehta Neal, is the IPO market different today in terms of listing markets compared with when you ran the largest small-cap market in the US?[37]

Neal Wolkoff Yes, it is different. I don't think any of the exchanges now really pay close attention, or focus on the small-cap market. There is also a dearth of attention from the investment banking sector on the small-cap market. It is difficult now for

---

[36] Some observers say the real reason Facebook went public is because it exceeded or bumped up against the 500-shareholder limit which would have required it to register with the Securities and Exchange Commission. The JOBS Act, as previously noted, raised the number of shareholders a company is allowed to have prior to being mandated to register to 2000 total, or 500 shareholders who are not accredited investors. "In other words," as Cheryl Knopp explained in a follow-up note, "Facebook didn't have enough control over its private shareholders in order to prevent them from simply transferring the shares. There were a lot of share transfers without the company being involved – and so it seemed like Facebook's shareholders became a lot of high-net worth individuals who were in it for the bump at IPO. They presumably would not be required to sign the underwriter lock up so they would be able to sell at the IPO."

Knopp added: "Contrast this with a large investment from an institution that wants to build a position. They buy a large amount pre-IPO and then likely will buy more at the IPO and hold the shares for a while. This is also arguably a more desirable shareholder base than lots of smaller individual shareholders."

[37] Referring to the American Stock Exchange where Wolkoff was Chairman and CEO from January 2005 to October 2008.

smaller companies to become public. There are other issues in the market that probably make it somewhat unattractive to go public. I give the Jobs Act credit for taking a stab at fixing this. Crowdfunding received all the press and was probably the most insignificant provision in the Jobs Act. It is, however, a million dollar limitation in the value of securities that can be bought and sold.[38] But that is just pointless for a company looking to go public, or to do crowdfunding. The limit is not realistic. If you are planning to go public you are not looking for just a million dollars.[39] You are looking for an investment banker too. There is also a loosening of other restrictions in the Jobs Act – in general solicitation[40] and in Section 404(b) of Sarbanes-Oxley Act of 2002.[41] These are not negligible.

Bookbinder I personally have a problem with the solicitation aspect of the Jobs Act. It exposes unsophisticated and retail investors to the opportunity for fraud and to be misinformed. I am not sure if you agree with that.

Wolkoff I don't. There are accredited and nonaccredited investors. I think most of the solicitations are limited to accredited investors.[42] I don't think that you can cherry-pick on one market that is dealing with the accredited investors and say, no you can't have any loosened restrictions – but then have other markets that are dealing with accredited investors that operate on a completely different plane. I have no

---

[38] See this section from: Jumpstart Our Business Startups Act: Frequently Asked Questions About Crowdfunding Intermediaries, Division of Trading and Markets, May 7, 2012: *Crowdfunding issuers.* Title III of the JOBS Act amends Section 4 of the Securities Act to create a new exemption for offerings of "crowdfunded" securities. Specifically, the JOBS Act amends Section 4 of the Securities Act to exempt issuers from the requirements of Section 5 of that Act when they offer and sell up to $1 million in securities, provided that individual investments do not exceed certain thresholds and the issuer satisfies other conditions in the JOBS Act, some of which will require rulemaking by the SEC." http://www.sec.gov/divisions/marketreg/tmjobsact-crowdfundingintermediariesfaq.htm

[39] As Wolfhoff explained in a follow-up: "Most companies don't go public for a million dollars, For some companies, yes, one million dollars of funding will work. But for others looking to go public, it is a drop in the bucket, not a replacement for going public."

[40] In a Fact Sheet, published July 10, 2013, the Securities and Exchange Commission explained: "While issuers will be able to widely solicit and advertise for potential investors, the JOBS Act required the SEC to adopt rules that require the issuer to take reasonable steps to verify that purchasers of the securities are accredited investors, using such methods as determined by the Commission." In other words, there is no restriction on who an issuer can solicit, but an issuer faces restrictions on who is permitted to purchase its securities." See http://www.sec.gov/news/press/2013/2013-124-item1.htm July 10, 2013.

[41] Section 404(b) of the Sarbanes-Oxley Act requires a publicly held company's auditor to attest to, and report on, management's assessment of its internal controls.

For more, see The JOBS ACT: A New IPO Playing Field for Emerging Growth Companies. Goodwin Procter April 25, 2012. http://www.goodwinprocter.com/Publications/Newsletters/Client-Alert/2012/0425_JOBS-ACT-A-New-IPO-Playing-Field-For-Emerging-Growth-Companies

[42] "Simply put, an accredited investor is someone who the SEC deems capable of taking on the economic risk of investing in unregistered securities. Entities may also be deemed accredited investors, including banks, partnerships, corporations, nonprofits and trusts." Source: Eric Rosenbaumm, *CNBC* website, February 4, 2015.

idea whether the Jobs Act will work, be amended, or be completely reformed. Public markets are, nevertheless, having a very difficult time when it comes to listing small-cap companies.

Bookbinder I don't disagree. That is the problem. Who is an accredited investor? You fill out your own form, and you hand it in. That is my personal concern – the advertising, the solicitation, who is an accredited investor, what should they see, what should someone else see? That part of the Jobs Act I personally have issues with.

Wolkoff Typically, we are not looking at this – investments in private offerings – as very significant investments. An accredited investor is somebody who says they are an accredited investor. Are you being defrauded when you defraud yourself? I don't think so. That is the difference. I look at people capable of making a distinction between lying to and telling their broker the truth. Either you are accredited or not. If you say you are accredited – and yet you are not – and then your broker goes through a legitimate process and takes the steps to determine if you are an accredited investor, then that should be good enough. On the other hand, if your broker has done nothing to make a determination then that may not be good enough. I don't know whether brokers will start wanting to do that under penalty and perjury with notaries and things like that. There has to be a point where people are allowed to make their own decisions. I know this is a controversial part of the law. I don't agree that people need to be as protected from themselves as your position would have it.

Mehta Let's say these companies go public and that now they are trading 10,000 or 100,000 shares a day. The Jobs Act also includes provisions to conduct a tick-size pilot study if the SEC decides that is warranted. Chris, what do you think of the comments from the last panel, the skepticism about the benefits from a pilot?[43] There was skepticism about five cents or even a dime increment spread bringing more liquidity back into the market – and about whether that would have any impact on research. How would a pilot be constructed? And what should not be in there? What types of tiers, what source of requirements should be in there for particular companies?

Concannon That is a pretty simple question (laughter). At first we need to look around the globe and at other markets that are fairly liquid and have different trading increments. Europe, for example, does adjust their tick sizes based on the company characteristics, both in its trading and in its market cap. I am still a bit concerned about yelling from the rafters, "Let's go back to nickels and fractions." I don't know if that approach delivers liquidity. But I do know that we have an overall liquidity problem in our less liquid names.

That is a macro problem. We are seeing equity trading volumes that are 30% off from what they were at their peak in recent years. And so the liquidity sitting in our market is probably more than 30% off. If you are trying to trade a stock, there are no

[43] Referring to a proposed pilot program for trading small-cap stocks in wider minimum increments. The pilot eventually was approved by the Securities and Exchange Commission. See SEC Approves Pilot Program to Assess Tick Size Impact for Smaller Companies. Center for Financial Stability, May 7, 2015. http://centerforfinancialstability.org/wp/?p=5987

market makers; there is no one committing capital; and there is no research. Maybe you shouldn't trade. Maybe it shouldn't be in your portfolio. If you look at the listing standards that we have today vs. the listing standards we had 10 years ago, it is an interesting study. You can go public without having profits. That wasn't the case 15 years ago when there were only certain markets that you could go public in.

Our current one-size-fits-all markets aren't working for a majority of our public companies, some of which shouldn't probably be public. I don't think it is just about tick size. There is a multitude of things we need to do around market structure that will help the buy-side move a large block of any illiquid stock.

The market that we have designed is great for the retail order flow – that is, 100, 200, 300 share trade sizes. It is efficient, it works, they get the best price, and the retail investor is price improved. But for the large block, say the 200,000 orders – and a stock that trades 10,000 shares a day – that is not easy to move without leaving a footprint.

Mehta What would you change? What else would be worth trying in a pilot to see if any of these things have an impact on the liquidity?

Concannon We should bring back the former New York Stock Exchange specialists (laughter). I am intrigued by the idea of exchanges having a monopoly around an illiquid name. But then I get scared because there was an exchange that once had a monopoly around both illiquid and liquid names and that didn't work.[44] When you have 13 exchanges and 40 or 50 dark pools today – I don't know what the count is anymore – we have a fragmentation issue when it comes to liquidity in names that aren't in one place.

I don't think we have a fragmentation issue in the top half of our equity markets. But I don't know how you control for fragmentation. The statute says we can trade stocks wherever we want to. That means the over-the-counter market can trade off an exchange. I don't know how you fix that. At the end of the day, we have a macro problem. Our economy sucks, our markets suck, and it is hard to trade in a market that sucks. I think I will put that in a comment letter to the SEC!

O'Brien That could be the tag line (laughter). Chris's comment about giving somebody a legal monopoly. When it comes to tick sizes, this might be a place to experiment. I have somewhat limited expectations. If you want any kind of assessment, you need to freeze as many different types of variables as possible. It needs to be uniform for both quoting and trading. It needs to be across the entire industry, not just exchanges. You have to go into it eyes wide open. Transaction costs by many measures will inevitably go up, and some of that will trickle back. Payment for order flow will go up for people who are internalizing retail flow at nickel spreads. It is something worth trying, because there are constituencies who feel like they are being ignored. It is a relatively low-impact way to try and test it out. There are limits to what we can do, but limited experimentation may be a reasonable expectation.

[44] Chris Concannon, tongue in cheek, is presumably referring here to the New York Stock Exchange on stock liquidity, and his reference to NYSE specialists points to their role on the floor prior to regulatory and technological changes that disintermediated human trader intervention. These human "specialists" were succeeded by (still human) Designated Market Makers, or DMMs, on the Big Board floor.

Mehta Neal, do you have any ideas for how to enhance liquidity in small-cap and large-cap stocks?

Wolkoff The idea of trying to hypothesize in advance what would work isn't quite as good as trying something on a pilot basis that does work. The Jobs Act as it is currently set up now is not a bad place to start. I am in favor of having some scheme of wider ticks. How you arrive at that I don't know. We should try different things. I kind of agree that at some point some of this is self-correcting when the economy returns to something resembling normal.

Concannon Less sucky!

Wolkoff Yeah, less sucky. I guess I will put it that way.

Concannon There is a nugget sitting inside the tick-size debate and that is called the "trade at."[45] We can change our quoting increments, to be sure, and Bill said it well, you have to change your trading increments so you can't trade within the spread. But that entire discussion about tick sizes will be sidetracked by the debate on the proposed "trade-at rule."

Mehta Any questions and comments from our audience?

Robert Schwartz Did I hear you ask the question, Nina, on how to get more liquidity into the small-cap market? An interesting way of creating more of this liquidity would be to introduce and strengthen the use of call auctions for these stocks. If memory serves properly, when trading in France moved to their new electronic continuous market they took all of the stocks at first and put them on a continuous electronic market. The less liquid half of those stocks just didn't work for them in terms of trading and liquidity. There was market failure in the continuous market space, and so they moved them back to call auctions.

Call auctions were the traditional way of trading in Paris before they introduced their electronic market. The call auctions worked very well. I also would like to repeat from the previous panel that the call auction is the same approach taken as AX Trading Group.[46] I have an association with AX Trading. I should disclose that. It is not easy starting a new operation to achieve critical mass; to get people's attention and even to get their understanding. But to me, I couldn't sit here quietly in the face of your question, when I am thinking that would be a very good way to generate more liquidity for small-cap stocks. I hope it would be a natural way, and that it would come about without requiring government regulation.

Grant Vingoe [Arnold & Porter LLP] With small-cap and mid-cap stocks, I have observed how a lot of foreign companies, just like US companies, are able to do private placements in the United States. And they remain fairly robust markets out-

[45] In a 2014 study, New York agency brokerage Rosenblatt Securities concluded that the introduction of a "trade-at" rule could halve trading volumes in US dark pools. The "trade at" would shift equity transactions onto lit exchanges unless dark pools or internalizing matching engines run by brokers could show notable price improvement had been accomplished.

[46] The AX Trading Group based in Stamford, Conn, is operator of the AX Trading Network. The company in early 2013 said it would shutter AX Trading, its dark pool share-trading platform, citing a slow pickup rate.

side of the US where they continue to trade freely. Those private placements can be sold in Canadian markets, for example. The differentiating factor tends to be the litigation environment, right? Those institutional investors and those private placements can take their lumps if these are speculative stocks. If a hedge fund loses money, it doesn't sue. In the foreign markets, there isn't the same class-action litigation environment. They aren't subject to the same enforcement risk. I don't know how to solve that problem. I would say the number one reason why US smaller companies would be deterred from going public today are the litigation and enforcement issues.

Bernard Donefer [Baruch College] Some days, our markets are highly correlated – stocks, options, futures, and to a lesser extent fixed income and foreign exchange. But we have multiple regulators: the SEC, FINRA and, in many cases now, we also have the Fed, and the Commodity Futures Trading Commission (CFTC). This was mentioned earlier today at this conference: Let's look at bad behavior and identify bad behavior consistently across multiple markets. Do we need a simplification of the regulatory infrastructures so that we can have that consistency across all markets and firms? Would that help?

O'Brien Are you focusing on achievable things here?

Concannon The answer is yes. Logically, you could have one regulator. Many countries have one regulator looking over all of those markets. You can get there without the political challenges through surveillance. It is just sharing data. There are some jurisdictional issues around sharing data, but it can simply be shared. There is more of that going on now than ever before since the Flash Crash in 2010. There has been an exchange of data across equities, options, and futures.

O'Brien I agree. Probably it doesn't matter if you have one regulator or 15. If they all have a complete picture, they are all heavily incentivized to spot the bad guys and chase them down.

Donefer The definition of bad guys? Flash trading was deemed illegal in equities.

O'Brien It never has, by the way.

Concannon Flash trading never was. Only Senator Charles Schumer deemed it illegal.[47]

Donefer You are absolutely right. But basically everybody stopped flash trading because it was such a controversial issue. However, flash trading still goes on in the options market – and so we have different sets of rules in asset classes as to what is bad behavior.

Mehta If we discuss flash trading, we may end up eating into the next speaker's time.

We have been there and it is too long of a discussion. Thank you all so very much.

---

[47] In a letter back in July 2009, Sen. Charles Schumer (D-NY) urged the SEC to ban flash order types. See Schumer Calls for Crackdown on 'Flash' Trading. http://www.forbes.com/2009/07/24/flash-trading-schumer-business-wall-street-flash.html

Chapter 8
History, Regulation, and the Evolution of a World-Class Exchange

Jeffrey Sprecher

Terry Martel [Baruch College] Jeffrey Sprecher is the perfect speaker to end this program today. As you know, Jeff is the founder, chairman, and CEO of Intercontinental Exchange. At ICE, he has done an outstanding job, from increasing its range of products in the energy markets to covering various other asset classes, such as agricultural credit and climate classes. Jeff has established four clearing houses, and several over-the-counter markets. And he has done this with a unique and trademark style. He is a dynamic leader. He is forceful yet collaborative, with a clear vision of the future and the character to execute on that vision for exchanges. Please welcome, Jeff Sprecher.

Sprecher On Friday, some major parts of Dodd-Frank will be enacted for the derivatives and the over-the-counter markets. This development is a priority for my company. I will talk about it later in the context of how regulation has evolved from the perspective of my company, and how it has done much to define it.

First, I want to take you back in time. I came out of the electric power industry.[1] In the 1980s, the United States was deregulating largely because consumers, particularly in California, wanted to have alternative energy plants, wind turbines, and solar panels. The monopoly of regulated utilities was not cooperating in the best interests of consumers. So governmental changes created electricity laws to permit private companies and private individuals to build power plants.[2] As deregulation evolved

[1] Sprecher went to work at Western Power Group in 1983 after meeting William Prentice at Sprecher's first job at Trane. Prentice was then developing power plants in the wake of industry deregulation.

[2] Significantly, deregulation in the electric industry was underway with enactment of the Energy Policy Act (1992).

J. Sprecher (✉)
Intercontinental Exchange (ICE), Atlanta, GA, USA

R.A. Schwartz et al. (eds.), *Rapidly Changing Securities Markets*,
Zicklin School of Business Financial Markets Series,
DOI 10.1007/978-3-319-54588-2_8

within the industry, you could eventually build large, central station power plants. In fact, if the regulation today would allow a private individual to build nuclear plants, and you could figure out how to permit that, then the industry would have come a very long way at the wholesale level to allow large independent power companies.

In any event, we were building these plants, and I stayed for 17 years at Western Power Group. These plants were financed a lot like apartment buildings or shopping malls. We would basically obtain a mortgage for about 90% of the value of the plant, usually borrowing in the bond market to do that. We would raise equity for 10% or so of the power plant.

We would set up as a partnership, my company as the general partner.

I was a major owner of Western Power Group. Over my 17-year career there, I eventually ended up with ownership in little tiny slugs of power plants all over the country. I wanted a market for the sale of electric power. We had a geographically diverse footprint, so the state of California again started taking a lead in deregulation. The state said, "Let's deregulate this market, but we don't know how to do it so we're going to address this important matter in public and private debate."

The state asked some people to sit on a panel to figure out how to deregulate.[3] There were three major electric utilities in California at the time: San Diego Gas and Electric in the south, Southern California Edison in Los Angeles in the north, and Pacific Gas and Electric Co. in San Francisco in the far north. These three were invited, along with a company called Enron.[4] Because Enron was then this larger-than-life entity that no one could describe, it was part of the emerging dot-com age. I was invited to represent independent power plants. I wanted to create a free market where we could trade electric power. It was for that reason that I started this company, the Intercontinental Exchange (ICE) in 2000.[5]

By the way, I lost that debate in California! California decided to do what the utilities wanted – build a government-run exchange. I kind of smiled to myself when I listened to this last panel here today, talking about how the cash equities business in the USA is kind of like a government-run exchange. Right? We have to ask permission to change something, to try something new. We can't pilot something without government approval. In the electric power industry there was that same view – we can't let the free market buy and sell electric power, we need this government-run exchange.

[3] 1996 is a significant other landmark year in deregulation in California. It was the year California began to ease controls on its energy sector in a move to stimulate more competition. The Electric Utility Industry Restructuring Act also became law.

[4] Enron Corporation was the famous US energy, commodities, and services company based in Houston, Texas, caught for accounting fraud and that went into bankruptcy on December 2, 2001.

[5] Today ICE owns, among other entities including futures and options entities, the NYSE and seven clearing houses. See https://www.intercontinentalexchange.com/about/overview

If you follow that chain of thought, the government-run exchange back in the day almost bankrupted the state of California.[6] It did bankrupt the largest utility in California. The governor was pushed out, so the state survived. However, the government's attempt to run that exchange really got California into trouble. So I left the state of California where I was living and created ICE outside the state. I figured there were 49 other states that were hopefully looking for a free-market solution.

Electric power trading was actual electrons being bought and sold between utilities, between power plant owners, and between grid operators. They were physically delivered contracts. In fact, no one thought of these as over-the-counter markets; no one thought of these as somehow trading markets. These were utilities doing what they did every day – operating power, which was why they were exchanging electrons. This was just 12 years ago, in 2000.

We then witnessed the emergence of Enron. Power trading was listed on the floor at the New York Mercantile Exchange (NYMEX). But we would see these constant market squeezes in the power trading markets. The reality is that, to deliver electrons, you must have access to a substation. And, to have access to a substation, you have to have a transmission line that is hooked to that substation. So we ended up with these nodes around the country. There would be four, five, or six electric utilities that had wires that came together – and that, in effect, offered them the opportunity to trade among each other.

These markets were prone to being squeezed, particularly after Enron started to buy wires and substations. I can say that now because it is not represented in this room! So my company organized the market and said: "Let's create cash settlement that doesn't have to be physically delivered. Let's find an index for each of these substations. We will just cash settle these contracts. We will widen the market beyond the four or five utilities."

I started ICE because I wanted to sell electrons. I didn't know anything about how to trade or run an exchange or anything. We designed version 1.0 of our trading platform, if you will, and we designed what is today called a central limit order book. We designed a platform where buyers and sellers would come together. It would operate on a FIFO[7] basis, and it matched market orders against the best bid or the best offer. It had no particular magic, no particular logic. We also started to drive the market toward standardizing, and we started to trade in units of energy to put things on that platform. We didn't know about contracts, so we traded electricity in terms of how many electrons you want. You know, how many megawatts of power do you want? We traded natural gas; so how many BTUs[8] do you want?

---

[6] History books recall the electricity blackouts among nearly 100,000 customers in California in the summer of 2000, and more blackouts in January 2001 when Governor Davis declared a state of emergency. San Diego Gas & Electric Company filed a complaint of manipulation of the markets during this "dark" chapter in the life of California.

[7] First in first out (FIFO) refers to the sequence of how trades are handled. In finance, it is an asset management and valuation method. The assets produced or purchased first are sold, used, or disposed of first.

[8] British thermal units.

This over-the-counter, or OTC, market that formed in the USA in the energy markets really was born out of a solely commercial transactional need, and we offered many delivery points. My company developed an agreement that said: "If you trade on our platform, here are all the rules." So we created the kind of things that ISDA[9] would normally do in the over-the-counter markets. We were never really thinking we were designing an OTC market in the way people think of it today.

Enron's collapse was the last major economic downturn in these developments. In my world, we subsequently got people to start using clearing arrangements because suddenly counterparty risk was a big concern. Once you start clearing, you can trade anonymously. Because you are looking to the clearing house as your counterparty, trading all of a sudden becomes standardized and anonymous. By the year 2002 (just a decade ago) in the energy markets, there was a central limit order book that was hooked to a clearing house that had standardized contracts traded anonymously.

A lot of the processes were automated during this period. At the same time, the incumbent exchanges, particularly the NYMEX which was my competitor, said: "Hey look at these guys over there, they are trading unregulated. They have this automated central limit order book system that looks a lot like what our futures exchange is that had this self-regulatory obligation we just talked about; and had all kinds of rules and a government relationship that we didn't have." There was increased pressure on my firm to start to look, act, and feel like a regulated exchange. In particular, around 2005, this was the subject of debate.

In 2006 there was a large company, a hedge fund called Amaranth.[10] It had 9.3 billion dollars in the natural gas market that blew up. It moved up the price of natural gas the day it blew up. So Senator Carl Levin, Chairman of the US Senate Permanent Subcommittee on Investigations, called a hearing.[11] He called me up and also called my colleague at NYMEX. A big picture of me appeared on the front of the *Financial Times* with one hand on a Bible and my other hand in the air. We testified that things were not going that well in this unregulated, over-the-counter market. It led to the government passing the Farm Bill, and we didn't fight it.[12] Actually, we helped craft it. And so, for the first time in the over-the-counter market, some

[9] The International Swaps and Derivatives Association, a trade association of banks and swap dealers. An "ISDA" is also shorthand for a type of protocol/contract they establish in more liquid OTC markets. See http://www2.isda.org/functional-areas/protocol-management/about-isda-protocols/

[10] Amaranth Advisors LLC was an American multistrategy hedge fund established by Nicholas Maounis, and headquartered in Greenwich, Connecticut. During its peak, the firm had up to 9 billion dollars in assets under management before collapsing in September 2006, after losing more than 5 billion dollars on natural gas futures. The firm's collapse was one of the largest known trading losses and hedge fund blow ups in history.

[11] See Amaranth Distorted Natural Gas Market, Senate Finds. Matthew Leising, *Bloomberg*, June 25, 2007. http://www.bloomberg.com/apps/news?pid=newsarchive&sid=aGgLCqUS9XCI

[12] The 2008 Farm Bill and regulations implemented by the Commodity Futures Trading Commission designated certain contracts as significant price discovery contracts. See also http://www.wsj.com/articles/SB118273168618646598

regulatory requirements were introduced, including position limits and large trade reporting. At the end of every day, we had to tell the government who all the large traders were, what their positions were, and so on. That effort morphed into the idea of, "hey, as long as we are covering this unregulated swaps market, we should also cover foreign companies that are doing business in the USA."

We all know that, in 2007 and 2008, we saw the mortgage-backed security business blow up too.[13] The risk was in instruments that were syndicated by the credit default swaps market all around the world. This, in my mind, is good risk management of syndicated risk. It brought down most of the Western economies in the process. But at least we didn't hold the entire risk in the USA. That is the way I always think about it, because we would really be in trouble otherwise. And that led to Dodd-Frank[14] which was signed into law in July 2010. That is the issue that is at the top of my mind today.

Title VII of Dodd-Frank[15] is the swaps regulation piece. It takes a number of things that were already happening with respect to my company and institutionalizes them into law. It requires that certain swaps be mandatorily cleared. It requires the reporting of positions. This is basically a way to create transparency, particularly for the government to see who is trading. Most interestingly, as it relates to this coming Friday, it determines who is a swaps dealer.

The definition of a swaps dealer is anybody who does 8 billion dollars' worth of notional business from a period that starts on this coming Friday and going forward. As soon as you start trading on Friday, you start calculating your total value of swaps. When you hit 8 billion dollars, you become a swaps dealer. What is a swaps dealer? A swaps dealer under Dodd-Frank will look a lot like a bank. It will have its capital ratios regulated. It will involve a lot more government oversight in general, and increased scrutiny of its behavior.

In the markets that we built – we really started these markets from scratch – they are not Wall Street dominated. The markets for energy in the USA are something that you would associate with Wall Street. In fact, they probably have only about 15% or so of their business conducted in the USA. Actually, 85% of the business is conducted by entities like the global conglomerate Louis Dreyfus Group, Shell Oil Company, or the multinational commodity trading and mining company Glencore that had its IPO this year. Those people think of themselves as owning grain elevators, warehouses, terminals, and trucks. They do not think of themselves as banks. They do not think that their capital ratios matter. They do not think of themselves as being systemically important. There is a big debate now about what will happen on

[13] Refers to the US subprime mortgage crisis, triggered by declines in US home prices that occurred with the US recession of December 2007 to June 2009.

[14] Formally known as The Dodd-Frank Wall Street Reform and Consumer Protection Act, Dodd-Frank was passed in response to the Great Recession, and it impacts all federal financial regulatory agencies and almost every aspect of the US financial services industry.

[15] See Dodd Dodd-Frank: Title VII – Wall Street Transparency and Accountability, https://www.law.cornell.edu/wex/dodd-frank_title_VII, Legal Information Institute.

Friday, when a lot of these energy and commodity merchants are suddenly faced with the prospect of being regulated in the USA.[16]

I have been receiving e-mails all day long because I have a team sitting in the lobby of the Commodities and Futures Trading Commission. There is a mob of people there today asking for clarifications, anything that they can throw at this to stop the freight train which is apparently coming on Friday. We took a look at it ourselves. And more than two years ago when Dodd-Frank was passed and being deliberated – before it was even legislation – we warned people on Capitol Hill that there would be some unintended consequences with Dodd-Frank. Two years ago, we began organizing this over-the-counter market I described, and that had been built on my system over the last ten years. We had been building internal systems to futurize, if you will, the over-the-counter markets.

If you trade a regulated future, there is no such thing as being a swaps dealer. We had been planning this for years. Once the totality of these Dodd-Frank rules started to permeate through the commodities and the derivatives markets, we announced what we were going to do. In fact, 100% of our customer base says: "We will follow you if you go there."

On Friday of this week we will operate our market for the last day as an over-the-counter market. On Monday, we will open for business as a futures market. We are transitioning all of our open positions from a regulatory umbrella that is now a regulated swaps business, to a regulated futures business. What does that mean? It means that from Monday forward anything that is traded on our platform will go across a real-time ticker. It will be completely transparent. It means that in order to be deemed a future, you will have to interface with a central limit order book. The bids and offers will be shown to everyone. It means that, for the first time, retail investors can trade in these markets.

Prior to this futurization, we were limited to market participants who had 100 billion dollars in assets as a minimum. It now means that brokers can participate in our markets. We have been operating under a "principals-only" regime.[17] That is where the buyers and sellers must push the button themselves to buy and to sell

[16] See Energy Markets Rev Up Dodd-Frank Compliance, Markets Media, October 1, 2012. http://marketsmedia.com/energy-markets-rev-up-dodd-frank-compliance/

The regulated trading of swaps by Dodd-Frank (in particular Title VII) required that certain SWAPS be traded on so-called electronic Swap Execution Facilities, or SEFs. Derivatives exchange, ICE, in summer 2012 began plans to overhaul trading in trillions of dollars of energy contracts, starting in January 2013, and in the process taking important steps ahead of the new financial regulations.

Commentators have noted that Title VII of Dodd-Frank was drafted based on the widely held view that the unregulated, bilateral (OTC) derivatives market was in large part a cause of the 2008 financial crisis.

[17] In recent years, the SEC had moved toward more "principles-based" regulation, in which regulatory guidance offers broad compliance principles, entrusting the regulated firms with applying those principles to their own circumstances. Historically, the SEC's rule-making has been "rules based," its regulations aiming to prescribe specific and detailed rules for reporting, or other obligations.

these swaps. In terms of the opacity in the OTC market, the market is saying, in effect, that it will give up that opacity in exchange for legal certainty of how to be viewed by government.

Shortly after we announced we would do this, other exchanges in the USA, including the Chicago Mercantile Exchange, announced they would try to futurize the interest rate swaps market. A competitor, for instance, has started the Eris Exchange,[18]announcing that it too is going to futurize the interest rate swaps markets.

What does all this mean? In my private conversations on Capitol Hill, particularly with the CFTC commissioners, they should declare their victory. If you would have said three or four years ago that we would take an entire asset class from the OTC market and make it all futures – put it on a real-time ticker with daily large trader reports, position limits, accountability, and complete transparency – people would say it couldn't be done. And if it could be done, wouldn't it be great?

Interestingly enough, that isn't how those people were looking at this. Most people said: "Wait a minute, we have built this elegant mouse trap. We have spent years debating these new things. We have new systems, new reports, and new pipes that have yet to be deployed. We're excited about it. And you guys have jumped right over them. You have gone from one extreme to another extreme."

But that is really just people who want to try out their new toy. It is looking at the trees and not at the forest. What we are seeing as a result is interesting. While the G20[19] says that we need a common set of global regulations for swaps, the reality is we haven't seen a regulator who wants to outsource local regulation to a foreign regulator. And so there is tremendous pressure to take global markets and dissect them and make them a series of regional markets – to balkanize the markets, so to speak.

We at ICE are now the largest exchange for trading oil. Oil trades are traded 24 hours a day. And this knows no boundaries. There is no logical home town for trading oil – and so it is very important for us. If there was, there would probably be a country where none of us would want to do business.

We are also seeing a lot of stress, or concern, on the part of our customers in Asia.[20] They are far away geographically from the USA. They don't really know what Dodd-Frank is. But they don't like what they hear. They have been coming out of the wood work over the last few weeks.

Nevertheless, our movement to futurize has helped to elevate a lot of those concerns. In just one decade it is quite interesting what has happed in this US energy market. It has been transformed from a physical, bilateral swaps market to a regulated futures market that is cash settled and cleared. In the process, that market has

[18] See Eris Exchange, http://www.erisfutures.com/

[19] The Group of Twenty, or G20, is the international forum for the governmental officials and central bank governors of 20 major economic powers.

[20] Comprehensive overview of the changes and major areas of concern contained in this presentation, OTC Derivatives and the Dodd-Frank Act, David Kaufman, David Lynn, March 9, 2011. Morrison Foerster http://media.mofo.com/files/Uploads/Images/110309-OTC-Derivatives-and-The%20Dodd-Frank-Act-Presentation.pdf

gone from being completely unregulated to being entirely regulated, at the highest form of regulation available for trading. It is an amazing success story. Not just my company, but a success story for a fledgling market to start up and then to go through this entire spectrum. All the shades of gray will end up with what I hope will be transparent, accessible, and reliable markets.

Finally, I want to comment on the process of going from being unregulated to being fully regulated. We have watched government as it relates to commodities in the USA: both from being relatively open to becoming basically principles based, to today becoming basically rules based.[21] It is the details in all of those rules that a lot of you guys in the securities industry, and a lot of the previous panels today, have been talking about – these fussy problems of trying to have a "one-size fits-all" set of rules in the equity space. You are increasingly seeing that morph into the commodities and derivatives space. There is this sense of how credit default swaps syndicated the risk of the commercial mortgage business and the retail mortgage business. I don't think that is a good thing for the next entrepreneur who will come along, trying to start and organize a market.

It will be increasingly more difficult than when my colleagues and I were, frankly speaking, just playing around in the late 1990s. Nonetheless, for the incumbent exchanges (and we are one), the fact that there will be a lot of fussy and finicky rules will create a lot of opportunity for innovation on how to operate within those rules. A slightly different kind of innovation, but an innovation that is probably available only to the incumbents.

I hope that on Monday of next week you will see press reports talking about the successful transformation of this market that we are operating on.[22] I will now take questions from the audience.

Kevin Callahan [AX Trading]. ICE has shown some interest in the cash equities exchange business. Is that some kind of recognition that your traditional business is now more regulated, and that you want to become a multi-asset exchange company? Most people, of course, are down on cash equities.

Sprecher We are not in the cash equities business. We acquired the rights to the Russell Indexes and have the Russell 2000 and 1000 value indices that trade as futures.[23] As a result of that, we have a number of algorithmic traders who operate in the cash equities space and who also arbitrage into the derivative space on our exchange. I don't rule anything in, or anything out. The cash equities space is complicated. That, I think, is a space for the big boys. I am not sure that I am that big.

---

[21] See footnote 16.

[22] See http://media.mofo.com/files/Uploads/Images/130716-Post-Dodd-Frank-Derivatives-Regulation.pdf

[23] ICE was not in the cash equities business at the time of this conference. However, as of writing in 2015, ICE is a significant player in the cash equities markets with its ownership of the New York Stock Exchange. Also, as of writing 2015, ICE will continue until 2017 to offer futures on the Russell 2000 and 1000 indices.

We have had a relatively successful time being incredibly opportunistic and entrepreneurial in my industry. I am sad to see that it has become harder to do that in the cash equities space. I don't know if I am particularly well suited for that, but we will see. I can't comment on anything because I am a public company. It is something we look at because we share some of your sympathy and pain.

Harold Bradley [Former Chief Investment Officer, Ewing Marion Kauffman Foundation]: There are a lot of charts that I look at reporting on banks, derivatives exposure, OTC swaps, and so on. After the Crash three years ago,[24] I expected to see a significant run down. Instead, there has been a symptomatic kind of rise in the total notional value of derivatives held by banks. This week I have been reading about Basel III.[25] And it seems that people think it's reducing it. I am not seeing any evidence of that overall. I'd like your comments, since you are running an exchange in a clearing house, on the total notional value of derivatives held by banks. The idea that it is all hedged doesn't seem to wash with me. Not when I look at the rise and the exposures. Could you address that?

Sprecher By way of background, after the Lehman collapse, I talked with US Treasury Secretary, Timothy Geithner,[26]and I worked with the Federal Reserve building the credit default swap (CDS) clearing house that took the CDSs off the books of the banks. We have been running it very successfully. I have a lot of views that came out of that experience.

First of all, the largest OTC asset class is interest rate swaps. Interest rate swaps are still largely not cleared. That notional value can really stack up. But, if you look at credit default swaps, the Fed put a lot of pressure on major banks. The nine largest banks in the world agreed voluntarily to begin clearing their credit default swaps. So far, since 2008, we have cleared 32 trillion dollars' worth of credit default swaps. What is interesting about this is the open interest. How much did that net down to? Under 2 trillion dollars. We put 32 trillion dollars in, and it resulted in 2 trillion dollars of true risk. The market in CDS is collapsing, that is to say, netting at the rate of 16 to 1.

Another way of looking at it is thinking about that fateful weekend in September 2008 when all these Wall Street guys were calling down to the Fed and were told Lehman Brothers is going down, and that you guys need to reach deep down into your pockets and save it. They all said: "I have no exposure to Lehman." What really existed was a chain of numerous trades. So it makes sense that they didn't think they had exposure. That is a pretty long chain that nobody, I think, realized existed. I would expect that the interest rate market has something similar. I would expect that it would collapse significantly when it is cleared.

---

[24] Refers to the financial crisis of 2007 and 2008 and the subsequent "Crash" on September 16, 2008, with the failures of major financial institutions in the US, including, most famously, Lehman Brothers. This occurred as a result of a chain of events blamed by analysts on toxic subprime loans.

[25] Basel III is the worldwide and voluntary regulatory framework on bank capital, stress testing, and market liquidity risk and ratios.

[26] Timothy (Tim) Geithner served as the 75th United States Secretary of the Treasury, under President Barack Obama, from 2009 to 2013.

I believe it helps that we own a clearing house. I am a strong advocate of clearing because it really collapses the risk. With respect to the collateral, there are a lot of big buy-side firms and *pundits* who say that it will soak up all the capital in the world to collateralize these derivatives. Right now, after the Lehman collapse, like you, I am hearing this from everybody: "I am fully collateralized. I am margining my customers and my customers are margining me. And I run a flat book." If you take that at face value, it suggests that there is 16 times more collateral in the world right now that is backing existing trades than would be necessary if it went into a clearing house.

Bradley Your thoughts on Basel III?

Sprecher It will be interesting to see the combination of that momentum moving to other asset classes, just like interest rate swaps becoming interest rate futures, and the capital charges of Basel. If you think about the story I wove, we started with a nascent market, standardized and cleared it, and applied regulation to it over a period of a decade as it was growing.

Can it be done all at once? It will not be as easy an evolution as the one I just spoke about. Depending on where those Basel charges shake out, it may become a sort of Big Bang Theory in the end. Thank you.

Kolibri 360 GmbH
Ferdinand-Jühlke-Straße 7
99095 Erfurt, Deutschland
produktsicherheit@kolibri360.de